SCHOLASTIC

W9-CFX-955

Cut, Paste & Write
ABC Activity Pages

by Tracy Jarboe and Stefani Sadler

NEW YORK • TORONTO • LONDON • AUCKLAND • SYDNEY
MEXICO CITY • NEW DELHI • HONG KONG • BUENOS AIRES

Teaching *Resources*

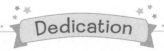

Dedication

We would like to dedicate this book to our
children, who have shaped our life with love—
Marisa, Jerry, Annalee, & Tomilyn
Heather & Josh

Scholastic Inc. grants teachers permission to photocopy the reproducible pages from this book for classroom use.
No other part of this publication may be reproduced in whole or in part, or stored in a retrieval system,
or transmitted in any form or by any means, electronic, mechanical, photocopying, recording, or otherwise,
without written permission of the publisher. For information regarding permission,
write to Scholastic Inc., 557 Broadway, New York, NY 10012.

Cover design by Jason Robinson
Interior design by Sydney Wright
Cover and interior art by Stefani Sadler

ISBN–13: 978-0-439-57630-7
ISBN–10: 0-439-57630-X

Copyright © 2006 by Tracy Jarboe and Stefani Sadler
Published by Scholastic Inc.

1 2 3 4 5 6 7 8 9 10   40   14 13 12 11 10 09 08 07 06

Contents

Introduction

Welcome to *Cut, Paste & Write ABC Activity Pages*—a collection of lessons for young learners that introduces and reinforces core literacy and math concepts in a fun, creative, and effective way.

An important aspect of literacy instruction in the early grades is to help children develop the understanding that letters of the alphabet correspond to certain sounds. Fostering this awareness among students helps create skilled and capable readers and writers. Research has shown that utilizing key picture and word associations to connect letters to sounds helps children establish this strong letter-sound foundation. As teachers, we can help children master this essential understanding by providing them with numerous experiences recognizing letters, writing letters, and associating sounds with letters. With this strong foundation in place, students will be on their way to reading and writing success!

We have also seen how active, hands-on learning that utilizes concrete materials and incorporates a variety of subject areas captivates students. They achieve a deeper and more meaningful understanding of concepts when they truly interact with their learning.

Using these guiding principles, we created 26 interactive lessons that creatively integrate literacy, mathematics, and art for young learners. The lessons use letters, sounds, key picture and word associations, shapes, and colors to provide children with valuable practice developing a range of fundamental skills. The stimulating combination of cross-curricular tasks includes:

* alphabet recognition
* letter-sound correspondence
* letter formation
* identifying positional and sight words
* identifying, matching, and locating geometric shapes
* classifying sizes of shapes
* identifying and utilizing colors

This book also helps develop and strengthen other important academic skills. As young learners face increasingly complex tasks, their oral language skills become more and more important. Strong oral language abilities produce capable, confident, and independent learners. These 26 lessons help improve oral language skills in students by providing them with repeated opportunities to listen, follow directions, question, and speak. Additionally, the actions found in these lessons, such as writing, coloring, cutting, gluing, and manipulating shapes, strengthen fine motor skills by emphasizing finger dexterity, wrist-hand-arm movement, and eye-hand coordination. Strong fine motor abilities enable students to perform a multitude of essential academic tasks.

The natural combination of art, math, and literacy in these 26 letter-by-letter lessons provides interesting, enjoyable, and extremely purposeful learning opportunities for all young learners!

What's Inside

Each letter-by-letter lesson features an alliterative theme and a corresponding poem and shape picture. For instance, the theme for *Aa* is *Ape with an Apple* and the lesson includes a poem and a shape picture about an ape with an apple. The lessons are organized into the following six sections:

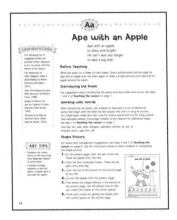

Before Teaching

Here you'll find a few suggested steps to complete in order to prepare for teaching the lesson.

Introducing the Poem

Each alphabet-inspired poem uses the alliterative theme of the lesson to introduce and highlight the focus letter and its corresponding sound(s). The poems all follow a similar four-line format, engaging young students with rhythm and rhyme while helping to develop their phonemic awareness. They also provide opportunities to incorporate movement into the lessons. Acting out the poems involves students in the learning process, and movement also creates wonderful opportunities for students to interact with one another. This section directs you to pages 6–7, which provide further ideas, steps, and examples for introducing the poem to your students.

Working with Words

Activate your students' background knowledge by helping them make connections between the focus letter's sound(s) and other words that begin with or possess the same sound(s). This section includes a list of suggested words that feature the focus letter and sound(s).

Shape Picture

This is the main activity of the lesson and gives children hands-on experience with literacy, math, and art tasks. Students use any of four shapes (squares, rectangles, triangles, and circles) to create pictures that relate to the overall theme of the lesson. This helps strengthen students' perceptual and spatial skills through tasks that require identifying, classifying, matching, locating, and representing shapes from different perspectives. Step-by-step instructions are also included, so that by examining students' pictures you will know how effectively they are following directions. In addition to coloring, cutting, and gluing, students practice writing uppercase and lowercase versions of the focus letter on lines provided beneath the pictures. Depending upon how you choose to manage the activity, students may complete the writing task before or after they complete the shape picture.

Art Tips

This section includes suggestions and helpful hints to enrich shape pictures, and also offers ideas for ways that students can personalize their work.

Literature Links

Titles that further expose students to the focus letter, its sound, and the theme of the lesson are listed in this section.

Using the ABC Activity Pages

Before Teaching

1. Rewrite the poem on chart paper. This exposes children to print and encourages them to follow along while you read. It also allows you to model appropriate reading behavior so that children begin to understand that:

   ✓ print carries meaning

   ✓ words are read top to bottom and left to right

   ✓ letters create particular sounds, and when joined together create words

   ✓ reading should be careful and even-paced, much like talking

   Decorating the poem with a photocopied activity page or simple drawings of the key picture associations also helps students connect letter to sound.

2. For certain lessons, decide upon which sounds you would like to focus.

   • Because vowels produce short and long sounds, each of the five vowel poems includes both sounds. You might want to discuss this fact with students at the start of each vowel lesson. Depending upon your teaching objectives, you might focus on one of the sounds or work with both sounds during a single lesson.

   • Certain consonants also produce more than one sound. To prevent confusion in these lessons (where young children might be less experienced with the additional consonant sounds), we focus on the hard sounds produced by words such as *cat* and *couch* in the Cc lesson and *goose* and *garden* in the Gg lesson.

3. Photocopy an activity and pattern page for each student using regular white copy paper.

4. Gather other materials to complete the picture: scissors, glue sticks or glue, and coloring materials such as crayons, colored pencils, or markers.

5. You may want to precut shapes using appropriately colored construction paper depending upon the abilities of your class.

6. Decide whether your students will work independently, in small groups, or as a whole class when completing the shape pictures and plan accordingly.

7. Select a suggested text from the **Literature Links** section if you would like to provide children with greater exposure to the focus letter, its sound, and the theme of the lesson.

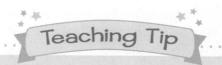

Teaching Tip

Depending upon the age and skill level of your students, consider pairing or grouping less experienced students with more experienced students. This assists in classroom management while allowing the more experienced children leadership opportunities and the less experienced children success in the learning process.

Teaching the Lesson

1. Introduce the focus letter of the lesson. Write the letter on a whiteboard or chart paper and ask students its name and corresponding sound. (If the letter is a vowel, you might discuss both the long and short sounds at this time.) Point out the formation of the uppercase and lowercase versions of this letter. Discuss appropriate writing strokes and tell students they will have a chance to practice writing both versions of the letter during the activity.

2. Read the alliterative poem to your students, focusing on the letter introduced and the sound it produces.

   • To help develop phonemic awareness in your students, draw attention to the alliteration (same initial sounds in succession) and the rhyme of the poem.

   • Ask children to identify other words in the poem that begin with the same sound as the focus letter. For instance in the "Cat on a Couch" poem (page 18), students could identify the words *cat*, *couch*, *cute*, *can*, *catching*, and *catnap* as words that possess the focus sound.

   • You might also challenge students to identify words that rhyme, such as *there* and *air* in "Bees by a Beehive" (page 16), or words that have same ending sound, such as *nest*, *night*, and *next* in "Nightingale in a Nest" (page 40).

   Encourage children to read the poem aloud with you. Practice reading until students can recite the poem together. This exposes students to important sight words and will help increase their confidence as readers! Also, consider incorporating movement into your introduction of the poem; for instance, "Walrus in the Water" (page 58) could be acted out as follows:

Walrus in the water,
   (use two index fingers to indicate tusks)

watching here and there.
   (hold opened hand above eyes, turning side to side)

While whales,
   (use hands above head to simulate spouting water)

seals,
   (clap hands as if they are flippers)

and fish
   (hold arms close to the body and flap hands to resemble fins)

swim in the ocean they all share!
   (join hands and sway side to side as if floating in the ocean)

3. Follow your introduction and discussion of the poem with the **Working with Words** activity. Access the background knowledge of students by asking them to create a list of other words that begin with the focus letter and possess the focus sound. You may want to create a word web, such as the example below, or you might write the words on sentence strips or index cards and add them to your word wall. (A list of suggested words accompanies each lesson).

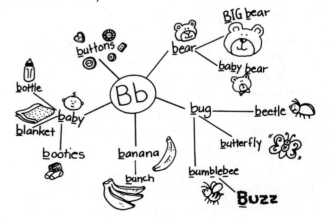

4. Each ABC activity page includes lines for students to practice writing the focus letter. Depending upon how you choose to manage the lesson, this can be completed before or after working on the shape picture. You may want to remind students of correct writing strokes before they begin writing and refer them to the guiding arrows to help them with directionality. Next, describe the activity to students:

- Highlight the names of the shapes and colors they will be working with during the lesson.

- Identify the activity page (which contains the writing task and shape picture) and the pattern page (which contains the shapes the students will be coloring, cutting, and gluing onto their pictures).

- Model the process of creating the shape picture by reading aloud and completing each step-by-step direction listed in the **Shape Picture** portion of the lesson page.

- Consider rewriting the steps on chart paper if appropriate for your class. This could be as simple as posting symbols to indicate the order of coloring, cutting, and gluing.

Discuss the importance of following directions with students. For the first project, you might want to model the entire process yourself, or you might have students join along and complete the project as a whole-class activity. For later projects, you might provide a completed shape project as an example; however, this can lead to less individual variability as students may attempt to mimic the example.

5. Once students are finished with the shape pictures and the letter writing, provide time for them to share their work with the rest of the class. Challenge them with questions such as:

- ▲ *What color is the rectangle?*

- ▲ *How many triangles?*

- ▲ *How many red triangles?*

- ▲ *How many more triangles than circles?*

- ▲ *What does the large triangle represent in the picture?*

- ▲ *Which shape is used the most?*

- ▲ *Which shape is used the least?*

- ▲ *What are some shapes you know that were not used?*

6. Provide more exposure to the focus letter, its sound, and the theme of the lesson by incorporating a suggested title from the **Literature Links** section. As you read, challenge students to identify words that possess the focus letter and sound.

7. Invite students to take their shape pictures home to share with family members!

Creating alphabet books is a wonderful way to use the completed shape projects. To do this, provide a folder for each student to collect his or her finished projects. Once students have finished all 26, bind the pages together and each child will have a book of A–Z shape pictures. Include the "My Alphabet Shape Book" Cover found on page 79 and invite children to decorate!

Extension Activities

The following list of purposeful and fun literacy-building activities can be used at any point before, during, or after a lesson to reinforce letter sounds:

✳ Sing the letter-name song each time a new letter is introduced. Use the tune from "Farmer in the Dell":

> *Horse starts with* Hh
> *Horse starts with* Hh
> *Hi-ho we all know*
> *Horse starts with* Hh

Alternatively, you might sing the letter-sound song:

> *Horse starts with* /h/
> *Horse starts with* /h/
> *Hi-ho we all know*
> *Horse starts with* /h/

✳ Sing the poems for each letter. Most of these poems lend themselves easily to simple tunes such as "Twinkle, Twinkle Little Star," "I'm a Little Teapot," or "Row, Row, Row Your Boat." You might also create your own tune or rhythmic chant.

✳ Chant the letter being introduced:

> */c/, /c/, car starts with* Cc
> *car, car starts with* Cc

Repeat the chant using another word that begins with the focus letter.

✳ When reading the poem for a lesson, invite students to perform an action each time they hear the focus letter's sound. Try several repetitions, changing the action each time. The students might clap their hands, snap their fingers, raise their hands, touch their noses, and so on.

✳ Give each child a tongue depressor with the focus letter written on one end. As you read the poem or a story from the **Literature Links** section, students can raise their letter sticks whenever they hear a word that begins with that focus letter's sound.

✳ Hold a scavenger hunt for things in the classroom whose names have the same initial sound as the focus letter of the lesson. For instance, during the *Bb* lesson students might identify a *backpack*, *ball*, *basket*, *book*, or *boots*.

✳ Set a timer for one, two, or three minutes and create a "Mad Minute List" of words that start with the focus letter. Students suggest words as you write them on chart paper or a whiteboard.

✳ Have the class remain seated and play "I Spy" with things around the classroom whose names have the same initial sound as the focus letter. For example, *I spy with my little eye something that starts with the /d/ sound.* The rest of the class can ask *yes* and *no* questions to guess the item.

✳ Collect books, newspapers, or magazines and encourage students to hunt for words or pictures that start with the focus letter and possess the focus sound of the lesson. If using newspapers and magazines, let students cut out the words and/or pictures and either create a class collage or individual collages for that letter. You might also have students copy words onto sentence strips and add them to your word wall.

✳ Dedicate a wall of the classroom to the focus letter and encourage students to decorate it with illustrations of items that begin with the focus letter and sound. For instance the Cc wall might have illustrations of a *cab*, *cage*, *camera*, *car*, *cat*, *coat*, *comb*, *computer*, *cookie*, *cracker*, or *cup*.

* Make a mystery letter window. Write the mystery letter on a small piece of paper. Using a brass fastener, attach a similar sized piece of paper printed with a question mark on top of the mystery letter paper. Provide clues about the mystery letter: *It is the 18th letter of the alphabet. It is the ending sound in the word* mother. *It is the beginning sound in the word* rabbit. Once students have identified the mystery letter, push aside the question mark paper to reveal the answer!

* Play a game in which students act out words that have the same initial sound as the focus letter of the lesson while the rest of the class guesses the word.

* Invite children to create the focus letter with their bodies!

* Students can make letter necklaces to wear when a new letter is introduced. Help students write the focus letter on an index card, punch two holes at the top of the card, and then string with yarn. Or you might create one on your own for students to take turns wearing throughout the day or week.

* Use large letter cutouts and tape and invite students to label objects in the classroom that begin with the featured letter, for example, *W* on the *window* or *whiteboard*. You might also use sentence strips to label the items.

* Ask students to trace the shape of the focus letter in the air while saying the sound that it makes. Have children trace it small, medium, and large.

* Invite students to decorate the focus letter. Print the letter on a piece of card stock and have students glue pasta, beads, buttons, or sequins on top.

* Students can form the focus letter using pipe cleaners, modeling clay, or, for a tasty treat, pretzel dough!

* Grow the focus letter. Fill an 8-inch square baking pan with soil. Students can observe as you trace the letter in the soil with your finger and then sprinkle grass seed in it. Next, gently cover the seed-filled letter with soil and, with your students' help, keep the soil moist. In about three days the focus letter will appear!

* Invite students to create focus letter wreaths. First help students cut out the center of a large paper plate. Then, let them glue on cutouts of the focus letter or pictures of things that begin with the focus letter.

* Students can make focus letter or alphabet chains. Distribute construction paper strips and ask students to label them with the focus letter or the different letters of the alphabet. Then show children how to use glue and loop the strips together to form a chain.

* Make a set of tactile letters with which students can practice finger tracing. Use glue to write a letter on a piece of card stock. Then sprinkle it liberally with glitter or sand, shake off the excess, and let it dry. Place the letter cards in a center and students can trace over them with their fingers or even make letter rubbings by placing a piece of paper on top and coloring.

* Create letter puzzles. Make a set of full-page-size letters on standard 8½- by 11-inch construction paper. Laminate and cut each letter into puzzle pieces. Store these letter puzzles individually in an envelope or a small plastic bag. Place them in a center for students to solve and discover the secret letter.

* Using a set of alphabet flashcards containing both uppercase and lowercase letter pairs, pass out one card to each student. (The number of cards used will depend upon the number of students in your class—for instance, in a class of 20 students, you would use only 10 letters of the alphabet, as each has an uppercase and lowercase card, for a total of 20 cards.) Once all students have one card, they must find the other student who is holding the matching uppercase or lowercase flashcard. An alternative approach would be to pass out lowercase cards to students and then hold up uppercase letters one at a time. Whichever student has the matching lowercase card reveals its name and the sound that it makes. You might even encourage students to share a word or two that begins with that letter.

* Create an alphabet basket. Draw a simple outline of a basket on construction paper. Divide the inside of the basket into 26 squares. Write all 26 uppercase letters in order on the squares inside the basket and laminate. Next, cut out 26 squares (sized to match the squares inside the basket) from white construction paper and write all lowercase letters on the squares. Finally, invite students to make an alphabet basket by placing the lowercase letters on top of their matching uppercase counterparts. Store the lowercase letters in a small plastic bag or tub.

* Give students small paper cups filled with alphabet pasta or cereal. Ask students to sort the letters. You might have them find as many of a particular letter as possible, or sort the letters according to various criteria—*Uppercase Letters, Lowercase Letters, Vowels, Consonants, "Sticks"* (letters made with all straight lines: *t, H, w*), *"Curves"* (letters made with all curved lines: *s, C, o*), *"Sticks and Curves"* (letters made with both straight and curved lines: *a, B, p*), and so on.

* Make an "alphabet soup." Give each child a paper or plastic bowl and a handful of letter manipulatives. Then, randomly call out alphabet letters one at a time. If students have the letter that has been called they place it in their bowls. The first student to fill his or her bowl and make a complete "alphabet soup" wins!

* Thoroughly clean and dry a clear 20-ounce plastic bottle. Pour a small set of alphabet beads, pasta, or cereal into the bottle and add colored sand to nearly fill the bottle. Use hot glue to secure the bottle cap. Make a recording sheet by writing all the letters of the alphabet on a sheet of paper. Have children shake and turn the bottle to see how many letters they can find. As students find letters, they can mark them on their recording sheets.

* Create an ABC class photograph book. Take a photograph of each of your students and as a class place them in alphabetical order: *Aa is for Anne*, *Bb is for Ben*, *Cc is for Chris and Carl*, and so on. If there are letters that do not have a student photo after them, consider including character names such as *Aa is for Arthur*, *Cc is for Clifford*, and so on.

* Make a class ABC book. Create a different page for each letter of the alphabet and invite students to draw items that begin with that letter. Students can decorate and label the pictures.

Connections to Early Childhood Standards

Language Arts

The activities in this book are designed to support you in meeting the following PreK–1 literacy goals and recommendations established in a joint position statement by the National Association for the Education of Young Children (NAEYC) and the International Reading Association (IRA)*:

* Participates in rhyming games
* Understands that print carries a message
* Engages in reading and writing attempts
* Recognizes letters and letter-sound matches
* Understands left-to-right and top-to-bottom orientation and basic concepts of print
* Begins to write letters of the alphabet

Source:

* *Learning to Read and Write: Developmentally Appropriate Practices for Young Children*, a joint position statement of the International Reading Association (IRA) and the National Association for the Education of Young Children (NAEYC). http://www.naeyc.org/about/positions/psread2.asp
© 1998 by the National Association for the Education of Young Children

Math

The activities also align with the following recommendations for the development of mathematical understanding and interest in young children established in a joint position statement by the National Association for the Education of Young Children (NAEYC) and the National Council of Teachers of Mathematics (NCTM)**:

* Begins to recognize, name, draw, compare, and sort 2-D shapes
* Describes size and orientation (for example: large triangle sitting on its point, small triangle sitting on its side)
* Describes object location with spatial words such as *on*, *in*, and *by*
* Uses shapes to create a picture

Source:

** *Early Childhood Mathematics: Promoting Good Beginnings*, a joint position statement of the National Association for the Education of Young Children (NAEYC) and the National Council of Teachers of Mathematics (NCTM). http://www.naeyc.org/about/positions/psmath.asp
© 2002 by the National Association for the Education of Young Children

Activity Pages

Aa

Ape with an Apple

Ape with an apple,
so shiny and bright!
He can't wait any longer
to take a big bite!

Literature Links

The following list of suggested books will provide further exposure to *Aa*, its sound, and the theme of the lesson:

The Adventures of Abby Alligator: Letter A (AlphaTales) by Maria Fleming (Scholastic, 2001)

Apes Find Shapes by Jane Belk Moncure (Children's Press, 1988)

Escape of Marvin the Ape by Caralyn & Mark Buehner (Dial Books, 1992)

Monkeys and Apes by Barbara Taylor (Peter Bedrick Books, 2002)

ART TIPS

▲ Students can create leaves on the tree using their fingertips dipped in green paint.

▲ Consider inviting students to add red glitter or glitter glue to decorate the apples.

Before Teaching

Write the poem on a sheet of chart paper. Glue a photocopied activity page for *Ape with an Apple* onto the chart paper or draw a simple picture of an ape and an apple around the poem.

Introducing the Poem

For suggestions about introducing the poem and focus letter and sound, see steps 1 and 2 of **Teaching the Lesson** on page 7.

Working with Words

After introducing the poem, ask students to brainstorm a list of additional words that begin with the letter *Aa* and possess the short or long *Aa* sounds. You might even create two lists—one for short-*a* words and one for long-*a* words (see examples below). Encourage children to be creative! For additional ideas, see step 3 of **Teaching the Lesson** on page 7.

short *Aa*: act, add, after, alligator, alphabet, animal, as, ask, at
long *Aa*: acorn, age, aim, ate

Shape Picture

For lesson and management suggestions, see steps 4 and 5 of **Teaching the Lesson** on page 8. Use the instructions below to direct students in completing the shape picture:

1. On the pattern page, color the two circles red. These are apples from the tree.

2. Color the four rectangles brown. These are the ape's arms and legs.

3. Color the rest of the picture on the activity page as you like.

4. Cut out the shapes from the pattern page.

5. Find where the shapes belong in the picture on the activity page. Use the dotted lines to help you match the shapes to the correct spaces.

6. Finish your project by gluing the shapes onto the correct spaces on the activity page.

Ape with an Apple

Trace and write.

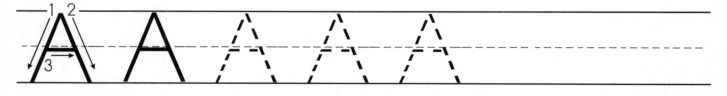

Bb

Bees by a Beehive

Bees by a beehive
buzzing here and there,
buzzing by the buttercups,
buzzing through the air!

Literature Links

The following list of suggested books will provide further exposure to *Bb*, its sound, and the theme of the lesson:

Bubble Bear: Letter B (AlphaTales) by Maxwell Higgins (Scholastic, 2001)

Buzz-Buzz, Busy Bees by Dawn Bentley (Little Simon, 2004)

Happy Bees by Arthur Yorinks (Harry N. Abrams, 2005)

Honeybee and the Robber by Eric Carle (Philomel Books, 1981)

Before Teaching

Write the poem on a sheet of chart paper. Glue a photocopied activity page for *Bees by a Beehive* onto the chart paper or draw a simple picture of bees and a beehive around the poem.

Introducing the Poem

For suggestions about introducing the poem and focus letter and sound, see steps 1 and 2 of **Teaching the Lesson** on page 7.

Working with Words

After introducing the poem, ask students to brainstorm a list of additional words that begin with the letter *Bb* and possess the *Bb* sound (see examples below). Encourage children to be creative! For additional ideas, see step 3 of **Teaching the Lesson** on page 7.

back, bad, bag, ball, balloon, bat, beach, bear, bed, bell, best, big, bike, bird, boat, book, bottle, bowl, boy, bread, bubble, bunny, bus

Shape Picture

For lesson and management suggestions, see steps 4 and 5 of **Teaching the Lesson** on page 8. Use the instructions below to direct students in completing the shape picture:

1. On the pattern page, color the two small circles yellow. These are the bees' heads.

2. Color the two medium circles yellow also. These are the bees' bodies.

3. Color the large circle black. This is the entrance to the beehive.

4. Color the rest of the picture on the activity page as you like.

5. Cut out the shapes from the pattern page.

6. Find where the shapes belong in the picture on the activity page. Use the dotted lines to help you match the shapes to the correct spaces.

7. Finish your project by gluing the shapes onto the correct spaces on the activity page.

ART TIPS

▲ Students can outline or fill in the beehive using strands of yellow yarn and glue. If filling in the beehive, it is helpful to glue the yarn in horizontal rows.

▲ Consider inviting students to add small black pom-poms to the end of each antenna or gluing glitter or birdseed to the center of each buttercup.

Bees by a Beehive

Trace and write.

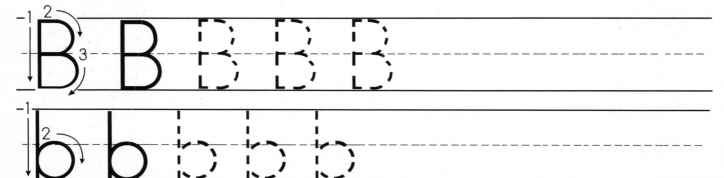

Cat on a Couch

Cat on a couch,
cute as can be,
catching a catnap
at half-past three!

Before Teaching

Write the poem on a sheet of chart paper. Glue a photocopied activity page for *Cat on a Couch* onto the chart paper or draw a simple picture of a cat and a couch around the poem.

Introducing the Poem

For suggestions about introducing the poem and focus letter and sound, see steps 1 and 2 of **Teaching the Lesson** on page 7.

Working with Words

After introducing the poem, ask students to brainstorm a list of additional words that begin with the letter Cc and possess the hard Cc sound (see examples below). Encourage children to be creative! For additional ideas, see step 3 of **Teaching the Lesson** on page 7.

cab, cage, camera, camp, can, car, coat, coin, comb, computer, cone, cookie, corn, cracker, cup

Shape Picture

For lesson and management suggestions, see steps 4 and 5 of **Teaching the Lesson** on page 8. Use the instructions below to direct students in completing the shape picture:

1. On the pattern page, color the medium circle orange. This is the cat's head.

2. Color the large circle orange. This is the cat's body.

3. Color the two rectangles any color. These are part of the couch.

4. Color the rest of the picture on the activity page as you like.

5. Cut out the shapes from the pattern page.

6. Find where the shapes belong in the picture on the activity page. Use the dotted lines to help you match the shapes to the correct spaces.

7. Finish your project by gluing the shapes onto the correct spaces on the activity page.

Literature Links

The following list of suggested books will provide further exposure to Cc, its sound, and the theme of the lesson:

Copycats: Letter C (AlphaTales) by Maria Fleming (Scholastic, 2001)

Cookie's Week by Cindy Ward (Putnam, 1988)

Have You Seen My Cat? by Eric Carle (F. Watts, 1973)

Sneakers the Seaside Cat by Margaret Wise Brown (HarperCollins, 2003)

ART TIPS

▲ Students can create patterns on the couch and/or the wall behind the cat. For example, they might create a pattern of stripes or dots. They can make the dots or stripes using their fingertips dipped in paint.

▲ Consider inviting students to glue a real button onto the couch pillow.

Cat on a Couch

Trace and write.

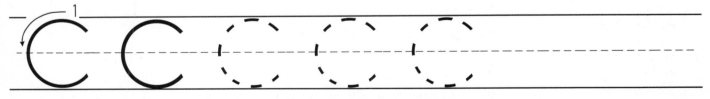

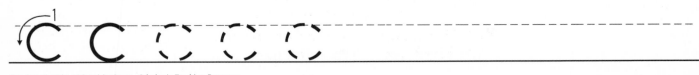

Dog in a Doghouse

Dog in a doghouse,
dreaming all alone,
of sitting in his doghouse
dining on a bone!

Before Teaching

Write the poem on a sheet of chart paper. Glue a photocopied activity page for *Dog in a Doghouse* onto the chart paper or draw a simple picture of a dog and a doghouse around the poem.

Introducing the Poem

For suggestions about introducing the poem and focus letter and sound, see steps 1 and 2 of **Teaching the Lesson** on page 7.

Working with Words

After introducing the poem, ask students to brainstorm a list of additional words that begin with the letter *Dd* and possess the *Dd* sound (see examples below). Encourage children to be creative! For additional ideas, see step 3 of **Teaching the Lesson** on page 7.

dad, dark, day, deck, deer, desk, dig, dime, dinosaur, dirt, dish, dive, doctor, doll, dolphin, donut, door, dragon, duck

Shape Picture

For lesson and management suggestions, see steps 4 and 5 of **Teaching the Lesson** on page 8. Use the instructions below to direct students in completing the shape picture:

1. On the pattern page, color the circle brown. This is the dog's head.

2. Color the two rectangles brown. These are the dog's legs.

3. Color the triangle red. This is the roof of the doghouse.

4. Color the rest of the picture on the activity page as you like.

5. Cut out the shapes from the pattern page.

6. Find where the shapes belong in the picture on the activity page. Use the dotted lines to help you match the shapes to the correct spaces.

7. Finish your project by gluing the shapes onto the correct spaces on the activity page.

ART TIP

Students can add a dog collar using a piece of yarn or ribbon and a small paper name tag. Have them punch a hole through the tag, string it onto the yarn or ribbon, and glue it around the neck of the dog. Students might even write the dog's name on the tag!

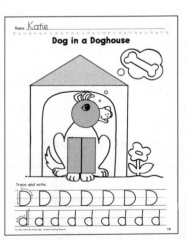

Dog in a Doghouse

Trace and write.

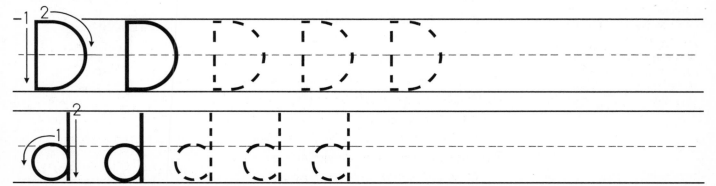

Eagle with an Egg

Eagle with an egg,
eager and excited,
expecting her eaglet,
she is delighted!

Literature Links

The following list of suggested books will provide further exposure to *Ee*, its sounds, and the theme of the lesson:

The Ballad of Blue Eagle by Steven E. Jones (Synergy Books, 2004)

The Enormous Elephant Show: Letter E (AlphaTales) by Liza Charlesworth (Scholastic, 2001)

Fly, Eagle, Fly!: An African Tale retold by Christopher Gregorowski (College Press, 2000)

Soaring with the Wind: The Bald Eagle by Gail Gibbons (Morrow Junior Books, 1998)

ART TIPS

▲ Students can glue strands of yellow yarn, straw, hay, or raffia onto the eagle's nest.

▲ Consider inviting students to add a thought bubble to the eagle to express her excitement!

Before Teaching

Write the poem on a sheet of chart paper. Glue a photocopied activity page for *Eagle with an Egg* onto the chart paper or draw a simple picture of an eagle and an egg around the poem.

Introducing the Poem

For suggestions about introducing the poem and focus letter and sound, see steps 1 and 2 of **Teaching the Lesson** on page 7.

Working with Words

After introducing the poem, ask students to brainstorm a list of additional words that begin with the letter *Ee* and possess the short or long *Ee* sounds. You might even create two lists—one for short-e words and one for long-e words (see examples below). Encourage children to be creative! For additional ideas, see step 3 of **Teaching the Lesson** on page 7.

short *Ee*: echo, edge, elbow, elf, elk, empty, energy, envelope, estimate, exercise
long *Ee*: each, ear, easel, east, eel, eleven, email, erase, evening

Shape Picture

For lesson and management suggestions, see steps 4 and 5 of **Teaching the Lesson** on page 8. Use the instructions below to direct students in completing the shape picture:

1. On the pattern page, color the two triangles brown. These are part of the eagle's wings.

2. Color the circle brown. This is the eagle's body.

3. Color the rest of the picture on the activity page as you like.

4. Cut out the shapes from the pattern page.

5. Find where the shapes belong in the picture on the activity page. Use the dotted lines to help you match the shapes to the correct spaces.

6. Finish your project by gluing the shapes onto the correct spaces on the activity page.

Name _____

Eagle with an Egg

Trace and write.

E E

e e

Frog by a Flower

Frog by a flower,
feeling just fine,
floating near his friends
in the bright sunshine!

Before Teaching

Write the poem on a sheet of chart paper. Glue a photocopied activity page for *Frog by a Flower* onto the chart paper or draw a simple picture of a frog and a flower around the poem.

Introducing the Poem

For suggestions about introducing the poem and focus letter and sound, see steps 1 and 2 of **Teaching the Lesson** on page 7.

Working with Words

After introducing the poem, ask students to brainstorm a list of additional words that begin with the letter *Ff* and possess the *Ff* sound (see examples below). Encourage children to be creative! For additional ideas, see step 3 of **Teaching the Lesson** on page 7.

fabric, falcon, family, farm, feather, fence, ferret, fig, finger, five, flag, flamingo, flea, flute, fly, food, fox, French fries, friend, fruit, fudge

Shape Picture

For lesson and management suggestions, see steps 4 and 5 of **Teaching the Lesson** on page 8. Use the instructions below to direct students in completing the shape picture:

1. On the pattern page, color the circle green. This is the frog's body.

2. Color the four triangles green. These are the frog's feet.

3. Color the rest of the picture on the activity page as you like.

4. Cut out the shapes from the pattern page.

5. Find where the shapes belong in the picture on the activity page. Use the dotted lines to help you match the shapes to the correct spaces.

6. Finish your project by gluing the shapes onto the correct spaces on the activity page.

ART TIPS

▲ Students can glue small pieces of colored tissue paper or glitter onto the flower's petals.

▲ Consider inviting students to add insects to the picture by drawing them on the activity page.

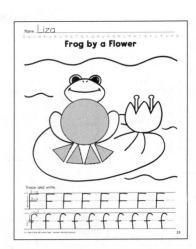

Frog by a Flower

Trace and write.

Goose in a Garden

Goose in a garden,
does grumble and groan.
Goose is so grouchy
because she is alone!

Literature Links

The following list of suggested books will provide further exposure to *Gg*, its sound, and the theme of the lesson:

Duck & Goose by Tad Hills (Schwartz & Wade Books, 2006)

Goose Moon by Carolyn Arden (Boyds Mills Press, 2004)

Goose's Story by Cari Best (Melanie Kroupa Books/Farrar, Straus and Giroux, 2002)

Gorilla, Be Good!: Letter G (AlphaTales) by Maria Fleming (Scholastic, 2001)

Before Teaching

Write the poem on a sheet of chart paper. Glue a photocopied activity page for *Goose in a Garden* onto the chart paper or draw a simple picture of a goose and a garden around the poem.

Introducing the Poem

For suggestions about introducing the poem and focus letter and sound, see steps 1 and 2 of **Teaching the Lesson** on page 7.

Working with Words

After introducing the poem, ask students to brainstorm a list of additional words that begin with the letter *Gg* and possess the hard *Gg* sound (see examples below). Encourage children to be creative! For additional ideas, see step 3 of **Teaching the Lesson** on page 7.

game, garage, garlic, gate, gazebo, ghost, glass, glitter, goat, goggles, gold, grain, granola, grapes, grass, gravel, gum

Shape Picture

For lesson and management suggestions, see steps 4 and 5 of **Teaching the Lesson** on page 8. Use the instructions below to direct students in completing the shape picture:

1. On the pattern page, leave the circle white. This is part of the goose's wing.

2. Color the square pink, red, or purple. This is part of the flower.

3. Color the two triangles orange. These are the goose's feet.

4. Color the rest of the picture on the activity page as you like (the goose may be left white).

5. Cut out the shapes from the pattern page.

6. Find where the shapes belong in the picture on the activity page. Use the dotted lines to help you match the shapes to the correct spaces.

7. Finish your project by gluing the shapes onto the correct spaces on the activity page.

ART TIP

Students can add dark clouds to the sky by rubbing a finger or cotton ball onto gray or black chalk and applying it to the activity page where appropriate. They can rub their fingers in circular motions to create billowy, dark clouds.

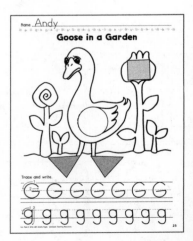

Goose in a Garden

Trace and write.

G G G G G

g g g g g

Horse by the Hay

Horse by the hay,
hip-hip-hooray!
He kicks up his heels,
horse is happy today!

Before Teaching

Write the poem on a sheet of chart paper. Glue a photocopied activity page for *Horse by the Hay* onto the chart paper or draw a simple picture of a horse and hay around the poem.

Introducing the Poem

For suggestions about introducing the poem and focus letter and sound, see steps 1 and 2 of **Teaching the Lesson** on page 7.

Working with Words

After introducing the poem, ask students to brainstorm a list of additional words that begin with the letter *Hh* and possess the *Hh* sound (see examples below). Encourage children to be creative! For additional ideas, see step 3 of **Teaching the Lesson** on page 7.

hair, half, hall, ham, hamburger, hammer, hamster, hand, hat, head, heart, helicopter, helmet, help, high, hill, hippo, home, hop, hotdog, house

Shape Picture

For lesson and management suggestions, see steps 4 and 5 of **Teaching the Lesson** on page 8. Use the instructions below to direct students in completing the shape picture:

1. On the pattern page, color the small circle brown. This is part of the horse's head.

2. Color the large circle brown. This is the horse's body.

3. Color the triangle black. This is the horse's tail.

4. Color the square brown. This is the horse's trough.

5. Color the rest of the picture on the activity page as you like.

6. Cut out the shapes from the pattern page.

7. Find where the shapes belong in the picture on the activity page. Use the dotted lines to help you match the shapes to the correct spaces.

8. Finish your project by gluing the shapes onto the correct spaces on the activity page.

Literature Links

The following list of suggested books will provide further exposure to *Hh*, its sound, and the theme of the lesson:

The Girl Who Loved Wild Horses by Paul Goble (Bradbury Press, 1978)

Hide-and-Seek Hippo: Letter H (AlphaTales) by Samantha Berger (Scholastic, 2001)

The Horse in Harry's Room by Syd Hoff (Harper & Row, 1970)

Horses! by Gail Gibbons (Holiday House, 2003)

ART TIP

Students can glue strands of yellow yarn, straw, hay, or raffia onto the hay in the horse's trough.

Horse by the Hay

Trace and write.

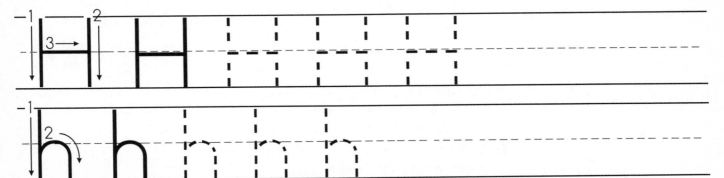

Iguana in the Ivy

Iguana in the ivy,
where he likes to be.
In the shady shadows,
impossible to see!

Literature Links

The following list of suggested books will provide further exposure to *Ii*, its sounds, and the theme of the lesson:

I Wanna Iguana by Karen Kaufman Orloff (Putnam, 2004)

The Iguana Brothers: A Tale of Two Lizards by Tony Johnston (Blue Sky Press, 1995)

Iguana on Ice: Letter I (AlphaTales) by Carol Pugliano-Martin (Scholastic, 2001)

The Night Iguana Left Home by Megan McDonald (DK, 1999)

ART TIP

Students can add texture to the ridges on the iguana's back by gluing sand onto the triangles.

Before Teaching

Write the poem on a sheet of chart paper. Glue a photocopied activity page for *Iguana in the Ivy* onto the chart paper or draw a simple picture of an iguana and ivy around the poem.

Introducing the Poem

For suggestions about introducing the poem and focus letter and sound, see steps 1 and 2 of **Teaching the Lesson** on page 7.

Working with Words

After introducing the poem, ask students to brainstorm a list of additional words that begin with the letter *Ii* and possess the short or long *Ii* sounds. You might even create two lists—one for short-*i* words and one for long-*i* words (see examples below). Encourage children to be creative! For additional ideas, see step 3 of **Teaching the Lesson** on page 7.

short *Ii*: if, igloo, ill, imagine, important, in, inch, inchworm, infant, insect, instrument
long *Ii*: ice, ice cream, idea, identical, iron, island

Shape Picture

For lesson and management suggestions, see steps 4 and 5 of **Teaching the Lesson** on page 8. Use the instructions below to direct students in completing the shape picture:

1. On the pattern page, color all four triangles green. Two of the triangles are part of the iguana and two of the triangles are part of the ivy.

2. Color the rest of the picture on the activity page as you like.

3. Cut out the shapes from the pattern page.

4. Find where the shapes belong in the picture on the activity page. Use the dotted lines to help you match the shapes to the correct spaces.

5. Finish your project by gluing the shapes onto the correct spaces on the activity page.

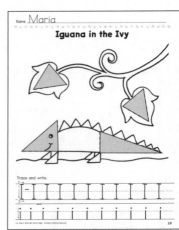

Iguana in the Ivy

Trace and write.

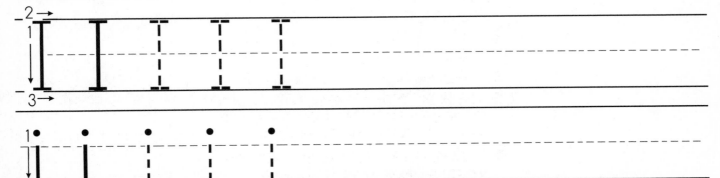

Jj

Jaguar in the Jungle

Jaguar in the jungle,
just wants to play.
He will jump for joy
when friends join him today!

Literature Links

The following list of suggested books will provide further exposure to *Jj*, its sound, and the theme of the lesson:

Jag by LeAnn Rimes (Penguin Group, 2003)

Jaguars by Ann O. Squire (Scholastic, 2005)

Jaguar's Jungleberry Jamboree: Letter J (AlphaTales) by Helen H. Moore (Scholastic, 2001)

Before Teaching

Write the poem on a sheet of chart paper. Glue a photocopied activity page for *Jaguar in the Jungle* onto the chart paper or draw a simple picture of a jaguar and a jungle around the poem.

Introducing the Poem

For suggestions about introducing the poem and focus letter and sound, see steps 1 and 2 of **Teaching the Lesson** on page 7.

Working with Words

After introducing the poem, ask students to brainstorm a list of additional words that begin with the letter *Jj* and possess the *Jj* sound (see examples below). Encourage children to be creative! For additional ideas, see step 3 of **Teaching the Lesson** on page 7.

jacket, jam, jar, jeans, jeep, jelly, jellybeans, jet, jewel, job, jog, joke, juggle, juice, July, jump, June, junk

Shape Picture

For lesson and management suggestions, see steps 4 and 5 of **Teaching the Lesson** on page 8. Use the instructions below to direct students in completing the shape picture:

1. On the pattern page, color the medium circle tan, gold, or light brown. This is part of the jaguar's head.

2. Color the large circle to match the color used for the medium circle. This is the jaguar's body.

3. Color the two rectangles to match the two circles. These are the jaguar's legs.

4. Color the rest of the picture on the activity page as you like.

5. Cut out the shapes from the pattern page.

6. Find where the shapes belong in the picture on the activity page. Use the dotted lines to help you match the shapes to the correct spaces.

7. Finish your project by gluing the shapes onto the correct spaces on the activity page.

ART TIP

Students can add black spots to the jaguar using a cotton swab dipped in black paint.

32

Jaguar in the Jungle

Trace and write.

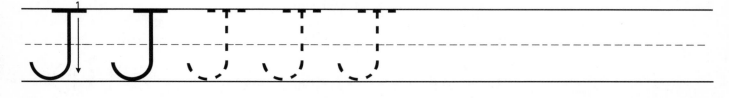

King with a Kite

King with a kite,
flying it so high,
above his kingdom
in the windy, windy sky!

ART TIP

Students can glue strands of yarn to the kite string or the kite tail.

Before Teaching

Write the poem on a sheet of chart paper. Glue a photocopied activity page for *King with a Kite* onto the chart paper or draw a simple picture of a king and a kite around the poem.

Introducing the Poem

For suggestions about introducing the poem and focus letter and sound, see steps 1 and 2 of **Teaching the Lesson** on page 7.

Working with Words

After introducing the poem, ask students to brainstorm a list of additional words that begin with the letter *Kk* and possess the *Kk* sound (see examples below). Encourage children to be creative! For additional ideas, see step 3 of **Teaching the Lesson** on page 7.

kabob, kangaroo, kayak, keep, kennel, ketchup, kettle, key, kick, kind, kindergarten, kiss, kitchen, kitten, kiwi, koala

Shape Picture

For lesson and management suggestions, see steps 4 and 5 of **Teaching the Lesson** on page 8. Use the instructions below to direct students in completing the shape picture:

1. On the pattern page, color the square yellow. This is the king's crown.

2. Choose two different colors for the four triangles. Use one color for two of the triangles and the other color for the two remaining triangles. These four triangles are the kite.

3. Color the rest of the picture on the activity page as you like.

4. Cut out the shapes from the pattern page.

5. Find where the shapes belong in the picture on the activity page. Use the dotted lines to help you match the shapes to the correct spaces.

6. Finish your project by gluing the shapes onto the correct spaces on the activity page.

King with a Kite

Trace and write.

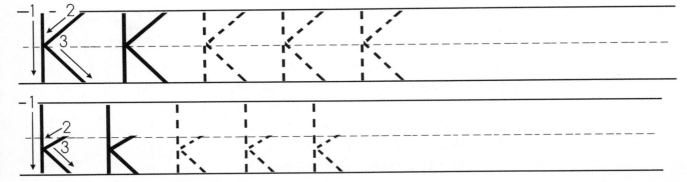

Ladybug on a Leaf

Ladybug on a leaf,
on six legs she stands.
Lucky little insect,
lunching where she lands!

Before Teaching

Write the poem on a sheet of chart paper. Glue a photocopied activity page for *Ladybug on a Leaf* onto the chart paper or draw a simple picture of a ladybug and a leaf around the poem.

Introducing the Poem

For suggestions about introducing the poem and focus letter and sound, see steps 1 and 2 of **Teaching the Lesson** on page 7.

Working with Words

After introducing the poem, ask students to brainstorm a list of additional words that begin with the letter *Ll* and possess the *Ll* sound (see examples below). Encourage children to be creative! For additional ideas, see step 3 of **Teaching the Lesson** on page 7.

lace, ladder, lake, lamp, land, late, leap, lemon, letter, life, lift, light, lime, lion, log, lollipop, long, look, luck, lunch

Shape Picture

For lesson and management suggestions, see steps 4 and 5 of **Teaching the Lesson** on page 8. Use the instructions below to direct students in completing the shape picture:

1. On the pattern page, color all four of the circles black. The largest circle is the ladybug's head. The three smaller circles are the ladybug's spots.

2. Color the rest of the picture on the activity page as you like.

3. Cut out the shapes from the pattern page.

4. Find where the shapes belong in the picture on the activity page. Use the dotted lines to help you match the shapes to the correct spaces.

5. Finish your project by gluing the shapes onto the correct spaces on the activity page.

ART TIPS

▲ Students can add a wiggle eye, or use a white crayon or colored pencil to draw an eye and/or smile onto the ladybug!

▲ Consider inviting students to add a small, black pom-pom nose to the ladybug.

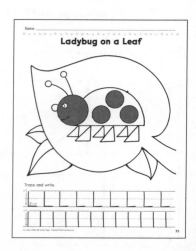

Ladybug on a Leaf

Trace and write.

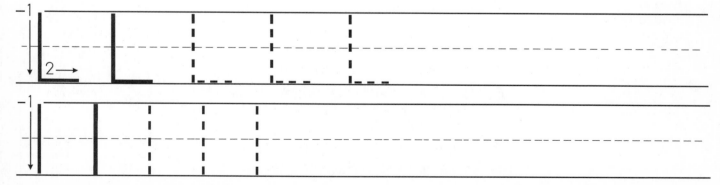

Mouse in a Meadow

Mouse in a meadow
in the merry month of May.
She might meet a friend
who can play with her today!

Literature Links

The following list of suggested books will provide further exposure to *Mm*, its sound, and the theme of the lesson:

If You Give a Moose a Muffin by Laura Numeroff (HarperCollins, 1991)

If You Give a Mouse a Cookie by Laura Numeroff (Harper & Row, 1985)

Monkey's Miserable Monday: Letter M (AlphaTales) by Valerie Garfield (Scholastic, 2001)

Mouse Count by Ellen Stoll Walsh (Harcourt Brace Jovanovich, 1991)

Before Teaching

Write the poem on a sheet of chart paper. Glue a photocopied activity page for *Mouse in a Meadow* onto the chart paper or draw a simple picture of a mouse and a meadow around the poem.

Introducing the Poem

For suggestions about introducing the poem and focus letter and sound, see steps 1 and 2 of **Teaching the Lesson** on page 7.

Working with Words

After introducing the poem, ask students to brainstorm a list of additional words that begin with the letter *Mm* and possess the *Mm* sound (see examples below). Encourage children to be creative! For additional ideas, see step 3 of **Teaching the Lesson** on page 7.

macaroni, mad, made, mail, make, man, map, marble, math, meal, meat, milk, mirror, mitten, monkey, moon, mop, morning, mouth, mud

Shape Picture

For lesson and management suggestions, see steps 4 and 5 of **Teaching the Lesson** on page 8. Use the instructions below to direct students in completing the shape picture:

1. On the pattern page, color the triangle gray. This is the mouse's face.

2. Color the medium circle yellow. This is the center of the flower.

3. Color the two small circles pink. These are the mouse's ears.

4. Color the rest of the picture on the activity page as you like.

5. Cut out the shapes from the pattern page.

6. Find where the shapes belong in the picture on the activity page. Use the dotted lines to help you match the shapes to the correct spaces.

7. Finish your project by gluing the shapes onto the correct spaces on the activity page.

ART TIPS

▲ Students can glue strands of black or gray yarn to the mouse's tail.

▲ Consider inviting students to add a small, black pom-pom nose to the mouse.

Mouse in a Meadow

Trace and write.

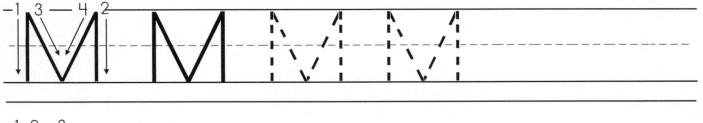

Nn

Nightingale in a Nest

Nightingale in a nest,
singing a goodnight song,
next to her new nestlings,
who sleep all night long!

Literature Links

The following list of suggested books will provide further exposure to *Nn*, its sound, and the theme of the lesson:

Best Nest by P. D. Eastman (Beginner Books, 1968)

My Nest Is Best by P. D. Eastman (Random House, 2005)

The Nicest Newt: Letter N (AlphaTales) by Heather Feldman (Scholastic, 2001)

The Nightingale adapted by Jerry Pinkney (Phyllis Fogelman Books, 2002)

ART TIPS

▲ Students can glue twigs, grass, or strands of yarn, straw, hay, or raffia to the nightingale's nest.

▲ Consider inviting students to add a wiggle eye to the nightingale.

Before Teaching

Write the poem on a sheet of chart paper. Glue a photocopied activity page for *Nightingale in a Nest* onto the chart paper or draw a simple picture of a nightingale and a nest around the poem.

Introducing the Poem

For suggestions about introducing the poem and focus letter and sound, see steps 1 and 2 of **Teaching the Lesson** on page 7.

Working with Words

After introducing the poem, ask students to brainstorm a list of additional words that begin with the letter *Nn* and possess the *Nn* sound (see examples below). Encourage children to be creative! For additional ideas, see step 3 of **Teaching the Lesson** on page 7.

nail, name, napkin, nature, neat, neck, needle, new, newspaper, next, nice, nickel, night, noon, north, nose, note, now, nurse, nut

Shape Picture

For lesson and management suggestions, see steps 4 and 5 of **Teaching the Lesson** on page 8. Use the instructions below to direct students in completing the shape picture:

1. On the pattern page, color the two circles black or brown. These are the head and body of the nightingale.

2. Color the two triangles to match the two circles. These are the nightingale's tail.

3. Color the rest of the picture on the activity page as you like.

4. Cut out the shapes from the pattern page.

5. Find where the shapes belong in the picture on the activity page. Use the dotted lines to help you match the shapes to the correct spaces.

6. Finish your project by gluing the shapes onto the correct spaces on the activity page.

Nightingale in a Nest

Trace and write.

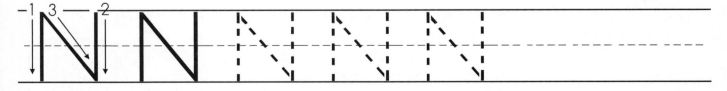

Octopus in the Ocean

Octopus in the ocean,
so timid and shy.
She only comes out
when a friend passes by!

Literature Links

The following list of suggested books will provide further exposure to *Oo*, its sounds, and the theme of the lesson:

My Very Own Octopus by Bernard Most (Harcourt Brace Jovanovich, 1980)

An Octopus Is Amazing by Patricia Lauber (Crowell, 1990)

Olive the Octopus's Day of Juggling: Letter O (AlphaTales) by Liza Charlesworth (Scholastic, 2001)

Oswald (Oswald Series) by Dan Yaccarino (Simon Spotlight/Nick Jr., 2004)

Before Teaching

Write the poem on a sheet of chart paper. Glue a photocopied activity page for *Octopus in the Ocean* onto the chart paper or draw a simple picture of an octopus and an ocean around the poem.

Introducing the Poem

For suggestions about introducing the poem and focus letter and sound, see steps 1 and 2 of **Teaching the Lesson** on page 7.

Working with Words

After introducing the poem, ask students to brainstorm a list of additional words that begin with the letter *Oo* and possess the short or long *Oo* sounds. You might even create two lists—one for short-o words and one for long-o words (see examples below). Encourage children to be creative! For additional ideas, see step 3 of **Teaching the Lesson** on page 7.

short *Oo*: object, October, olive, on, operate, opposite, ostrich, ox, oxygen
long *Oo*: oak, oatmeal, open, over, own

Shape Picture

For lesson and management suggestions, see steps 4 and 5 of **Teaching the Lesson** on page 8. Use the instructions below to direct students in completing the shape picture:

1. On the pattern page, color four of the octopus's legs one color and the remaining four another color.

2. Color the rest of the picture on the activity page as you like.

3. Cut out the shapes from the pattern page.

4. Find where the shapes belong in the picture. Use the dotted lines to help you match the shapes to the correct spaces.

5. Make a pattern with the octopus legs, for example, pink, blue, pink, blue, and so on.

6. Finish your project by gluing the shapes onto the correct spaces on the activity page.

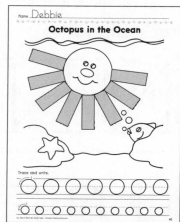

ART TIPS

▲ Students can add "suction cups" to the legs of the octopus using fingertips dipped in white paint.

▲ Consider inviting students to add glue dots to the air bubbles, and sand or glitter to the ocean floor.

Name _____

Octopus in the Ocean

Trace and write.

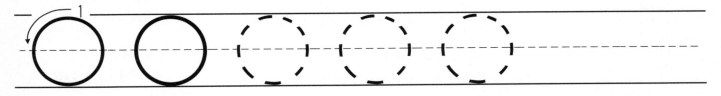

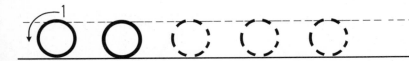

Pig in a Puddle

Pig in a puddle,
playing all day!
Covered in mud,
Piggy likes it that way!

Literature Links

The following list of suggested books will provide further exposure to *Pp*, its sound, and the theme of the lesson:

If You Give a Pig a Pancake by Laura Numeroff (Laura Geringer Books, 1998)

If You Give a Pig a Party by Laura Numeroff (Laura Geringer Books, 2005)

Piggie Pie! by Margi Palatini (Clarion Books, 1995)

The Pigs' Picnic: Letter P (AlphaTales) by Helen H. Moore (Scholastic, 2001)

ART TIP

Students can glue a curled pipe cleaner or a strand of yarn curled in a spiral to the pig's tail.

Before Teaching

Write the poem on a sheet of chart paper. Glue a photocopied activity page for *Pig in a Puddle* onto the chart paper or draw a simple picture of a pig and a puddle around the poem.

Introducing the Poem

For suggestions about introducing the poem and focus letter and sound, see steps 1 and 2 of **Teaching the Lesson** on page 7.

Working with Words

After introducing the poem, ask students to brainstorm a list of additional words that begin with the letter *Pp* and possess the *Pp* sound (see examples below). Encourage children to be creative! For additional ideas, see step 3 of **Teaching the Lesson** on page 7.

pack, pad, paint, paper, pat, pen, penny, people, picture, pie, pillow, please, pond, pull, pumpkin, puppet, puzzle

Shape Picture

For lesson and management suggestions, see steps 4 and 5 of **Teaching the Lesson** on page 8. Use the instructions below to direct students in completing the shape picture:

1. On the pattern page, color the circle pink. This is the pig's snout.

2. Color the four rectangles pink. These are the pig's legs.

3. Color the rest of the picture on the activity page as you like.

4. Cut out the shapes from the pattern page.

5. Find where the shapes belong in the picture on the activity page. Use the dotted lines to help you match the shapes to the correct spaces.

6. Finish your project by gluing the shapes onto the correct spaces on the activity page.

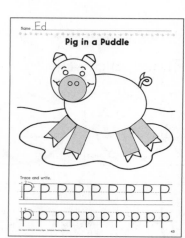

44

Pig in a Puddle

Trace and write.

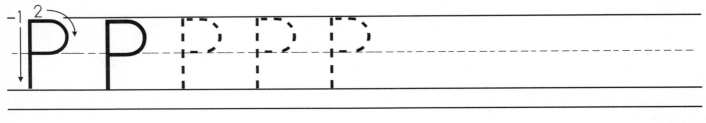

Qq

Quail on a Quilt

Quail on a quilt,
quietly walking by.
When she wants to hurry,
quite quickly she will fly!

Literature Links

The following list of suggested books will provide further exposure to *Qq*, its sound, and the theme of the lesson:

Keeping Quilt by Patricia Polacco (Simon & Schuster, 1988)

Quail Song: A Pueblo Indian Folktale by Valerie Scho Carey (Putnam, 1990)

Quail's Egg: A Folk Tale from Sri Lanka by Joanna Troughton (Bedrick/Blackie, 1988)

The Quiet Quail: Letter Q (AlphaTales) by Heather Feldman (Scholastic, 2001)

Before Teaching

Write the poem on a sheet of chart paper. Glue a photocopied activity page for *Quail on a Quilt* onto the chart paper or draw a simple picture of a quail and a quilt around the poem.

Introducing the Poem

For suggestions about introducing the poem and focus letter and sound, see steps 1 and 2 of **Teaching the Lesson** on page 7.

Working with Words

After introducing the poem, ask students to brainstorm a list of additional words that begin with the letter *Qq* and possess the *Qq* sound (see examples below). Encourage children to be creative! For additional ideas, see step 3 of **Teaching the Lesson** on page 7.

quack, quake, quarrel, quart, quarter, queen, question, quick, quiet, quit, quiz

Shape Picture

For lesson and management suggestions, see steps 4 and 5 of **Teaching the Lesson** on page 8. Use the instructions below to direct students in completing the shape picture:

1. On the pattern page, color the triangle gray or brown. This is the quail's tail.

2. Pick two colors for the four squares. Use one color for two of the squares and the other color for the remaining two squares. These are the corners of the quilt.

3. Color the rest of the picture on the activity page as you like.

4. Cut out the shapes from the pattern page.

5. Find where the shapes belong in the picture on the activity page. Use the dotted lines to help you match the shapes to the correct spaces.

6. Finish your project by gluing the shapes onto the correct spaces on the activity page.

ART TIPS

▲ Students can glue buttons or fabric pieces onto their quilts.

▲ For added fine motor-skill practice, consider inviting students to punch holes in the quilt, lace strands of yarn through the holes, and tie the strands in a knot.

Quail on a Quilt

Trace and write.

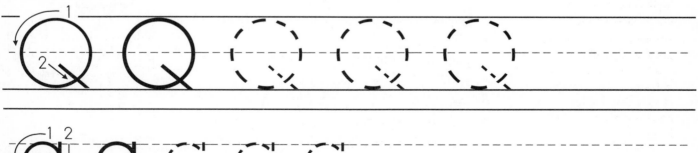

Rr
Rabbit by a River

Rabbit by a river,
resting in the sun.
Race back to your rabbit hole,
run, run, run!

Before Teaching

Write the poem on a sheet of chart paper. Glue a photocopied activity page for *Rabbit by a River* onto the chart paper or draw a simple picture of a rabbit and a river around the poem.

Introducing the Poem

For suggestions about introducing the poem and focus letter and sound, see steps 1 and 2 of **Teaching the Lesson** on page 7.

Working with Words

After introducing the poem, ask students to brainstorm a list of additional words that begin with the letter *Rr* and possess the *Rr* sound (see examples below). Encourage children to be creative! For additional ideas, see step 3 of **Teaching the Lesson** on page 7.

race, radio, rag, rain, rainbow, rat, red, rest, rich, ride, right, ring, road, rocket, room, rope, rose, rug, ruler

Shape Picture

For lesson and management suggestions, see steps 4 and 5 of **Teaching the Lesson** on page 8. Use the instructions below to direct students in completing the shape picture:

1. On the pattern page, color the two triangles pink. These are the rabbit's ears.

2. Color the two circles so that they match one another. You can choose between white, gray, or brown. These are the rabbit's hind leg and tail.

3. Color the rest of the picture on the activity page as you like.

4. Cut out the shapes from the pattern page.

5. Find where the shapes belong in the picture on the activity page. Use the dotted lines to help you match the shapes to the correct spaces.

6. Finish your project by gluing the shapes onto the correct spaces on the activity page.

Literature Links

The following list of suggested books will provide further exposure to *Rr*, its sound, and the theme of the lesson:

Bunny Cakes by Rosemary Wells (Dial Books, 1997)

My Friend Rabbit by Eric Rohmann (Roaring Brook Press, 2002)

Rosie Rabbit's Radish: Letter R (AlphaTales) by Wendy Cheyette Lewison (Scholastic, 2001)

Runny Babbit: A Billy Sook by Shel Silverstein (HarperCollins, 2005)

ART TIPS

▲ Students can glue a cotton ball to the rabbit's tail

▲ Consider inviting students to add wiggle eyes to the rabbit.

Rabbit by a River

Trace and write.

Seahorse in the Sea

Seahorse in the sea,
loves to swim and play!
Smiling at the sea stars,
she nods and says, "Good Day!"

Before Teaching

Write the poem on a sheet of chart paper. Glue a photocopied activity page for *Seahorse in the Sea* onto the chart paper or draw a simple picture of a seahorse and the sea around the poem.

Introducing the Poem

For suggestions about introducing the poem and focus letter and sound, see steps 1 and 2 of **Teaching the Lesson** on page 7.

Working with Words

After introducing the poem, ask students to brainstorm a list of additional words that begin with the letter *Ss* and possess the *Ss* sound (see examples below). Encourage children to be creative! For additional ideas, see step 3 of **Teaching the Lesson** on page 7.

sad, safe, salt, sandwich, saw, seed, sell, sing, sit, sky, small, snow, soap, sock, son, song, sound, steak, sun, surf

Shape Picture

For lesson and management suggestions, see steps 4 and 5 of **Teaching the Lesson** on page 8. Use the instructions below to direct students in completing the shape picture:

1. On the pattern page, color the two triangles purple. These are the fins on the back of the seahorse.

2. Color the two circles pink. These are the head and body of the seahorse.

3. Color the rest of the picture on the activity page as you like.

4. Cut out the shapes from the pattern page.

5. Find where the shapes belong in the picture on the activity page. Use the dotted lines to help you match the shapes to the correct spaces.

6. Finish your project by gluing the shapes onto the correct spaces on the activity page

Seahorse in the Sea

Trace and write.

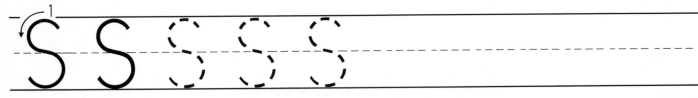

Turtle Under a Tree

Turtle under a tree,
tapping her tiny toes.
She is humming a tune
that only turtles know!

Literature Links

The following list of suggested books will provide further exposure to *Tt*, its sound, and the theme of the lesson:

One Tiny Turtle by Nicola Davies (Candlewick Press, 2001)

Tammy Turtle: A Tale of Saving Sea Turtles by Suzanne Tate (Nags Head Art, 1991)

Turtle Bay by Saviour Pirotta (Farrar, Straus, and Giroux, 1997)

When Tilly Turtle Came to Tea: Letter T (AlphaTales) by Carol Pugliano-Martin (Scholastic, 2001)

ART TIP

Students can decorate the sun with gold glitter or glitter glue.

Before Teaching

Write the poem on a sheet of chart paper. Glue a photocopied activity page for *Turtle Under a Tree* onto the chart paper or draw a simple picture of a turtle and a tree around the poem.

Introducing the Poem

For suggestions about introducing the poem and focus letter and sound, see steps 1 and 2 of **Teaching the Lesson** on page 7.

Working with Words

After introducing the poem, ask students to brainstorm a list of additional words that begin with the letter *Tt* and possess the *Tt* sound (see examples below). Encourage children to be creative! For additional ideas, see step 3 of **Teaching the Lesson** on page 7.

table, tag, tail, take, talk, tall, tape, teach, team, teeth, ten, tie, time, toad, toe, toy, tub, tune, TV

Shape Picture

For lesson and management suggestions, see steps 4 and 5 of **Teaching the Lesson** on page 8. Use the instructions below to direct students in completing the shape picture:

1. On the pattern page, color the square brown. This is part of the turtle's shell.

2. Color the triangle green. This is the top of the tree.

3. Color the rectangle brown. This is the trunk of the tree.

4. Color the circle yellow. This is part of the sun.

5. Color the rest of the picture on the activity page as you like.

6. Cut out the shapes from the pattern page.

7. Find where the shapes belong in the picture on the activity page. Use the dotted lines to help you match the shapes to the correct spaces.

8. Finish your project by gluing the shapes onto the correct spaces on the activity page

Turtle Under a Tree

Trace and write.

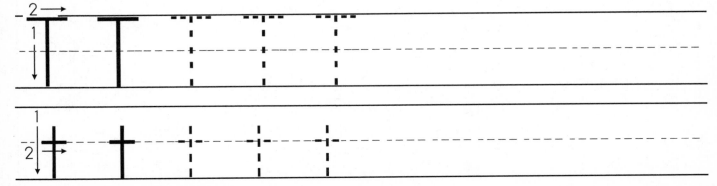

Unicorn Under an Umbrella

Unicorn under an umbrella,
upset there is no sun.
She will have to wait,
until she can have more fun!

Literature Links

The following list of suggested books will provide further exposure to *Uu*, its sound, and the theme of the lesson:

I Wished for a Unicorn by Robert Heidbreder (Kids Can Press, 2000)

Umbrella by Taro Yashima (Viking Press, 1958)

Umbrellabird's Umbrella: Letter U (AlphaTales) by Heather Feldman (Scholastic, 2001)

Where Have the Unicorns Gone? by Jane Yolen (Simon & Schuster, 2000)

ART TIPS

▲ Students can create a cloudy sky by rubbing an index finger or cotton ball on gray or black chalk and applying it to the sky.

▲ Consider using eyedroppers with several colors of paint to drop paint onto the umbrella.

Before Teaching

Write the poem on a sheet of chart paper. Glue a photocopied activity page for *Unicorn Under an Umbrella* onto the chart paper or draw a simple picture of a unicorn and an umbrella around the poem.

Introducing the Poem

For suggestions about introducing the poem and focus letter and sound, see steps 1 and 2 of **Teaching the Lesson** on page 7.

Working with Words

After introducing the poem, ask students to brainstorm a list of additional words that begin with the letter *Uu* and possess the short or long *Uu* sounds. You might even create two lists—one for short-*u* words and one for long-*u* words (see examples below). Encourage children to be creative! For additional ideas, see step 3 of **Teaching the Lesson** on page 7.

short Uu: umpire, uncle, under, upset, until, unusual
long Uu: uniform, unique, unit, United States, use, useful, usual

Shape Picture

For lesson and management suggestions, see steps 4 and 5 of **Teaching the Lesson** on page 8. Use the instructions below to direct students in completing the shape picture:

1. On the pattern page, leave the small triangle and circle white. These are the horn and head of the unicorn.

2. Color the square black. This is the hoof of the unicorn.

3. Color the medium triangle any color. This is part of the umbrella.

4. Color the rest of the picture on the activity page as you like.

5. Cut out the shapes from the pattern page.

6. Find where the shapes belong in the picture on the activity page. Use the dotted lines to help you match the shapes to the correct spaces.

7. Finish your project by gluing the shapes onto the correct spaces on the activity page.

Unicorn Under an Umbrella

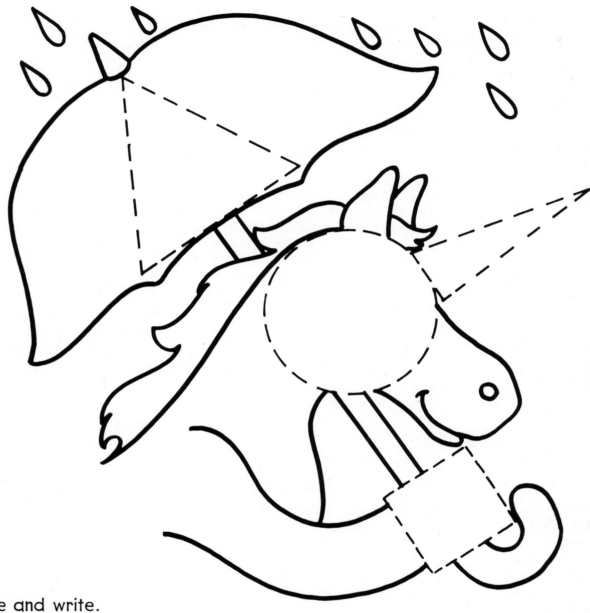

Trace and write.

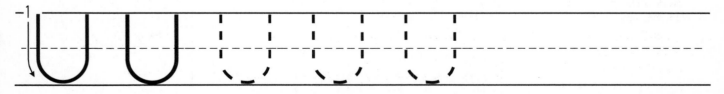

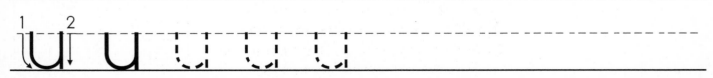

Viper on a Vine

Viper on a vine,
doesn't make a sound.
He is very clever
and very rarely found!

Literature Links

The following list of suggested books will provide further exposure to *Vv*, its sound, and the theme of the lesson:

The Day Jimmy's Boa Ate the Wash by Trinka Hakes Nobel (Dial Press, 1980)

Vera Viper's Valentine: Letter V (AlphaTales) by Maxwell Higgins (Scholastic, 2001)

Verdi by Janelle Cannon (Harcourt Brace, 1997)

The Viper by Lisa Thiesing (Puffin Books, 2002)

ART TIP

Students can decorate the picture with glitter or glitter glue. For example, they can outline the squares with gold glitter or give the viper a red glitter tongue and eyes.

Before Teaching

Write the poem on a sheet of chart paper. Glue a photocopied activity page for *Viper on a Vine* onto the chart paper or draw a simple picture of a viper and a vine around the poem.

Introducing the Poem

For suggestions about introducing the poem and focus letter and sound, see steps 1 and 2 of **Teaching the Lesson** on page 7.

Working with Words

After introducing the poem, ask students to brainstorm a list of additional words that begin with the letter *Vv* and possess the *Vv* sound (see examples below). Encourage children to be creative! For additional ideas, see step 3 of **Teaching the Lesson** on page 7.

vacation, vacuum, valentine, van, vanilla, vase, vegetable, velvet, very, video, village, violin, visit, voice, volume, vowel

Shape Picture

For lesson and management suggestions, see steps 4 and 5 of **Teaching the Lesson** on page 8. Use the instructions below to direct students in completing the shape picture:

1. On the pattern page, color the four squares yellow. These are part of the viper's body.

2. Color the triangle green. This is the viper's head.

3. Color the rest of the picture on the activity page as you like.

4. Cut out the shapes from the pattern page.

5. Find where the shapes belong in the picture on the activity page. Use the dotted lines to help you match the shapes to the correct spaces.

6. Finish your project by gluing the shapes onto the correct spaces on the activity page.

Viper on a Vine

Trace and write.

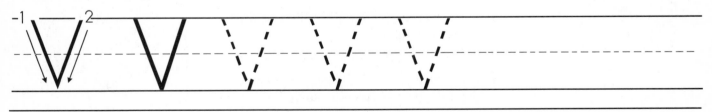

Walrus in the Water

Walrus in the water,
watching here and there.
While whales, seals, and fish swim
in the ocean they all share!

Before Teaching

Write the poem on a sheet of chart paper. Glue a photocopied activity page for *Walrus in the Water* onto the chart paper or draw a simple picture of a walrus and water around the poem.

Introducing the Poem

For suggestions about introducing the poem and focus letter and sound, see steps 1 and 2 of **Teaching the Lesson** on page 7.

Working with Words

After introducing the poem, ask students to brainstorm a list of additional words that begin with the letter *Ww* and possess the *Ww* sound (see examples below). Encourage children to be creative! For additional ideas, see step 3 of **Teaching the Lesson** on page 7.

wag, wagon, walk, wall, want, wasp, watch, weather, web, week, west, when, whisper, wig, window, wing, wood, work, worm

Shape Picture

For lesson and management suggestions, see steps 4 and 5 of **Teaching the Lesson** on page 8. Use the instructions below to direct students in completing the shape picture:

1. On the pattern page, leave the two triangles white. These are the tusks of the walrus.

2. Color the two circles pink. These are part of the walrus' face.

3. Color the rest of the picture on the activity page as you like.

4. Cut out the shapes from the pattern page.

5. Find where the shapes belong in the picture on the activity page. Use the dotted lines to help you match the shapes to the correct spaces.

6. Finish your project by gluing the shapes onto the correct spaces on the activity page.

Literature Links

The following list of suggested books will provide further exposure to *Ww*, its sound, and the theme of the lesson:

Little Walrus Warning by Carol Young (Soundprints, 1996)

Wally the Lost Baby Walrus by Chris Kiana (Publication Consultants, 1999)

Walruses by Charles Rotter (Child's World, 2001)

Worm's Wagon: Letter W (AlphaTales) by Samantha Berger (Scholastic, 2001)

ART TIPS

▲ Students can add a line of blue glitter or glitter glue along the scallops of water.

▲ Consider adding wiggle eyes to the animals in the ocean.

Walrus in the Water

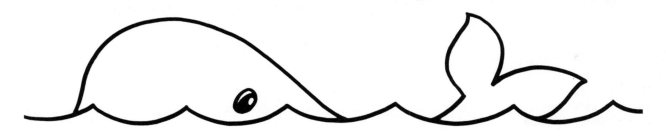

Trace and write.

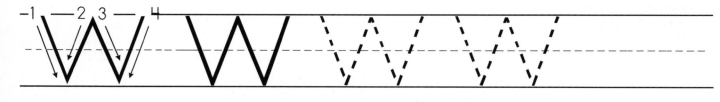

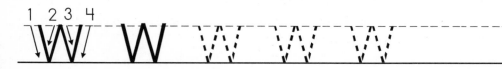

Fox in a Box

Fox in a box,
learned some new tricks.
He practiced very well,
now he can do six!

Literature Links

The following list of suggested books will provide further exposure to *Xx*, its sound, and the theme of the lesson:

Fox in Socks by Dr. Seuss (Beginner Books, 1965)

Hattie and the Fox by Mem Fox (Bradbury Press, 1986)

Rosie's Walk by Pat Hutchins (Macmillan, 1967)

A Xylophone for X-Ray Fish: Letter X (AlphaTales) by Liza Charlesworth (Scholastic, 2001)

Before Teaching

Write the poem on a sheet of chart paper. Glue a photocopied activity page for *Fox in a Box* onto the chart paper or draw a simple picture of a fox and a box around the poem.

Introducing the Poem

For suggestions about introducing the poem and focus letter and sound, see steps 1 and 2 of **Teaching the Lesson** on page 7.

Working with Words

After introducing the poem, ask students to brainstorm a list of additional words that contain the letter *Xx* and possess the *Xx* sound (see examples below). Encourage children to be creative! For additional ideas, see step 3 of **Teaching the Lesson** on page 7.

ax, example, excellent, excuse, exercise, mix, next, ox, relax, six, taxi, x-ray

Shape Picture

For lesson and management suggestions, see steps 4 and 5 of **Teaching the Lesson** on page 8. Use the instructions below to direct students in completing the shape picture:

1. On the pattern page, color the smallest triangle orange or red. This is the fox's snout.

2. Color one of the medium triangles to match the small triangle. This is part of the fox's tail.

3. Leave the other medium triangle white. This is the tip of the fox's tail.

4. Color the square yellow. This is part of the box.

5. Color the rest of the picture on the activity page as you like.

6. Cut out the shapes from the pattern page.

7. Find where the shapes belong in the picture on the activity page. Use the dotted lines to help you match the shapes to the correct spaces.

8. Finish your project by gluing the shapes onto the correct spaces on the activity page.

ART TIPS

▲ Students can create a name for the fox and write it on the box.

▲ Consider adding wiggle eyes and/or a pom-pom nose to the fox.

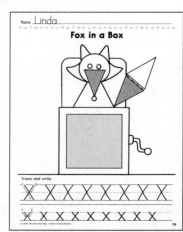

Fox in a Box

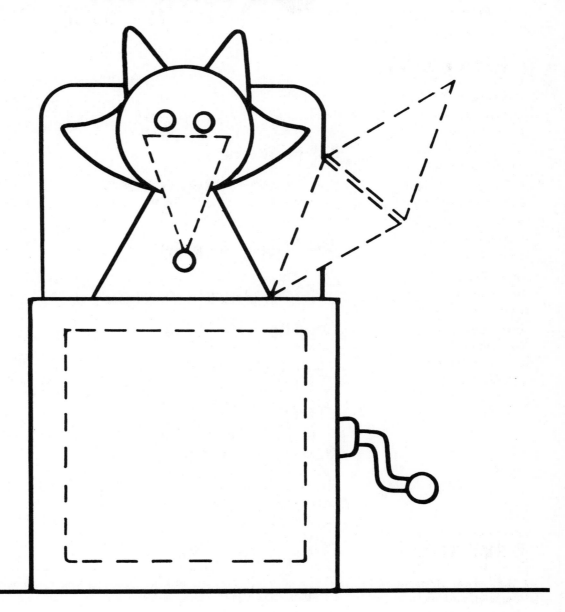

Trace and write.

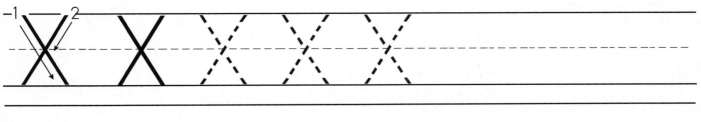

Yak in the Yard

Yak in the yard,
eats and eats all day.
He is always hungry
for yummy yellow hay!

Literature Links

The following list of suggested books will provide further exposure to *Yy*, its sound, and the theme of the lesson:

Bob and Jack: A Boy and His Yak by Jeff Moss (Bantam Books, 1992)

Go Track a Yak by Tony Johnston (Simon & Schuster, 2003)

The Yak Who Yelled Yuck: Letter Y (AlphaTales) by Carol Pugliano-Martin (Scholastic, 2001)

ART TIPS

▲ Students can add wiggle eyes and black dots for nostrils to the yak.

▲ Consider gluing strands of yellow yarn, straw, hay, or raffia onto the haystack and the hay in the yak's mouth.

Before Teaching

Write the poem on a sheet of chart paper. Glue a photocopied activity page for *Yak in the Yard* onto the chart paper or draw a simple picture of a yak and a yard around the poem.

Introducing the Poem

For suggestions about introducing the poem and focus letter and sound, see steps 1 and 2 of **Teaching the Lesson** on page 7.

Working with Words

After introducing the poem, ask students to brainstorm a list of additional words that begin with the letter *Yy* and possess the *Yy* sound (see examples below). Encourage children to be creative! For additional ideas, see step 3 of **Teaching the Lesson** on page 7.

yacht, yam, yardstick, yarn, yawn, year, yell, yellow, yes, yesterday, yodel, yogurt, you, young, yucky, yummy

Shape Picture

For lesson and management suggestions, see steps 4 and 5 of **Teaching the Lesson** on page 8. Use the instructions below to direct students in completing the shape picture:

1. On the pattern page, color the square brown. This is the yak's snout.

2. Color the rectangle blue. This is the door of the house.

3. Color the triangle black. This is the roof of the house.

4. Color the rest of the picture on the activity page as you like.

5. Cut out the shapes from the pattern page.

6. Find where the shapes belong in the picture on the activity page. Use the dotted lines to help you match the shapes to the correct spaces.

7. Finish your project by gluing the shapes onto the correct spaces on the activity page.

Yak in the Yard

Trace and write.

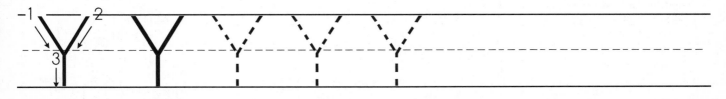

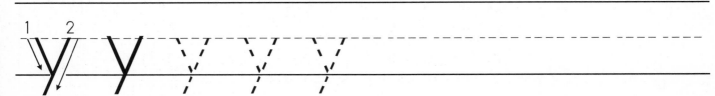

Zz

Zebra at the Zoo

Zebra at the zoo,
looking quite cute!
All zipped up
in a black and white suit.

Before Teaching

Write the poem on a sheet of chart paper. Glue a photocopied activity page for *Zebra at the Zoo* onto the chart paper or draw a simple picture of a zebra and a zoo sign around the poem.

Introducing the Poem

For suggestions about introducing the poem and focus letter and sound, see steps 1 and 2 of **Teaching the Lesson** on page 7.

Working with Words

After introducing the poem, ask students to brainstorm a list of additional words that begin with the letter *Zz* and possess the *Zz* sound (see examples below). Encourage children to be creative! For additional ideas, see step 3 of **Teaching the Lesson** on page 7.

zap, zero, zigzag, zip, zipper, zip code, ziti, zone, zoom, zucchini

Shape Picture

For lesson and management suggestions, see steps 4 and 5 of **Teaching the Lesson** on page 8. Use the instructions below to direct students in completing the shape picture:

1. On the pattern page, leave the small square white. This is the zebra's snout.

2. Color the large square brown. This is the zebra's trough.

3. Color the triangle black. This is the zebra's tail.

4. Color the rest of the picture on the activity page as you like.

5. Cut out the shapes from the pattern page.

6. Find where the shapes belong in the picture on the activity page. Use the dotted lines to help you match the shapes to the correct spaces.

7. Finish your project by gluing the shapes onto the correct spaces on the activity page

Literature Links

The following list of suggested books will provide further exposure to *Zz*, its sound, and the theme of the lesson:

On Beyond Zebra!
by Dr. Seuss (Random House, 1955)

Zach the Lazy Zebra: Letter Z (AlphaTales) by Wendy Cheyette Lewison (Scholastic, 2001)

Zebras by Melissa Stewart (Children's Press, 2002)

Zella, Zack, and Zodiac by Bill Peet (Houghton Mifflin, 1986)

ART TIPS

▲ Students can add a wiggle eye to the zebra.

▲ Consider gluing strands of thin black yarn to the zebra's mane and tail.

Zebra at the Zoo

Trace and write.

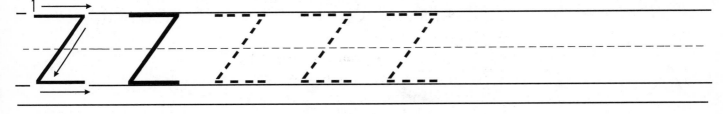

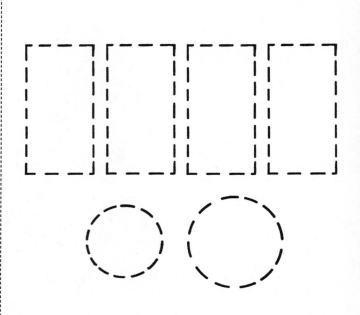

Bees by a Beehive   Bb

Bees by a Beehive   Bb

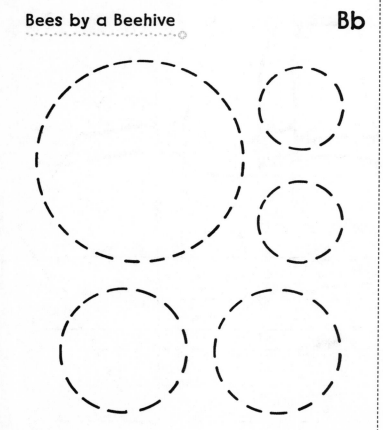

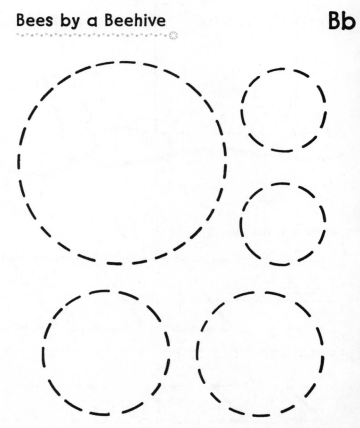

Dog in a Doghouse   Dd

Dog in a Doghouse   Dd

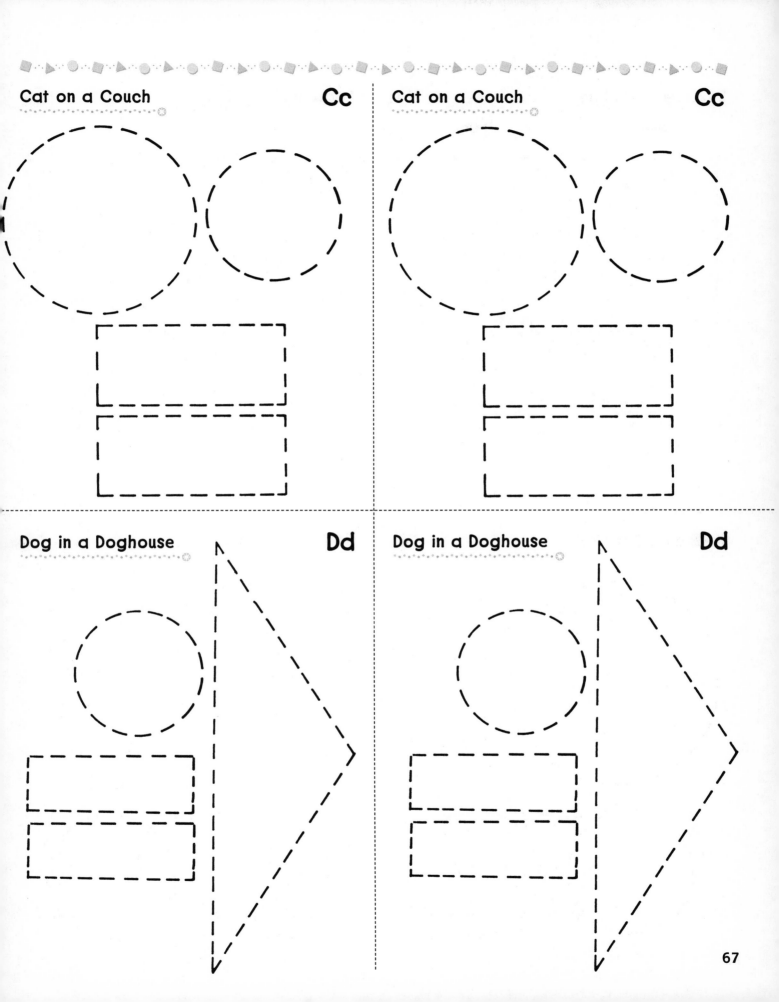

Eagle with an Egg

Ee

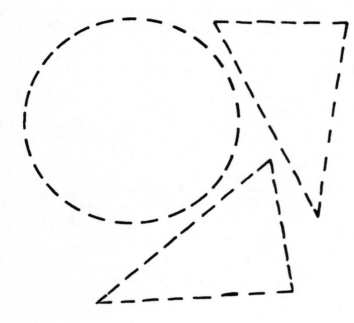

Eagle with an Egg

Ee

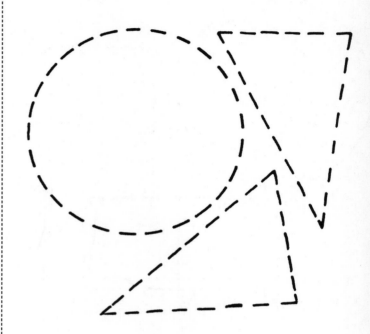

Frog by a Flower

Ff

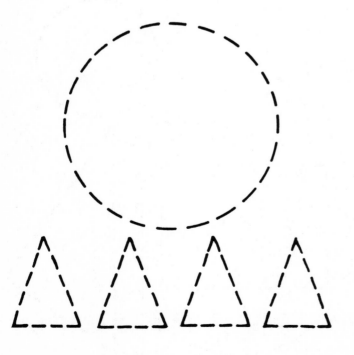

Frog by a Flower

Ff

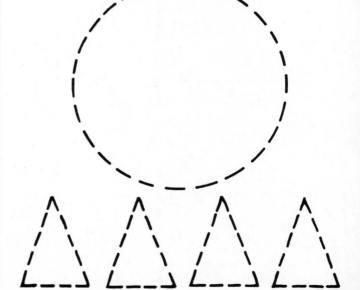

Goose in a Garden

Gg

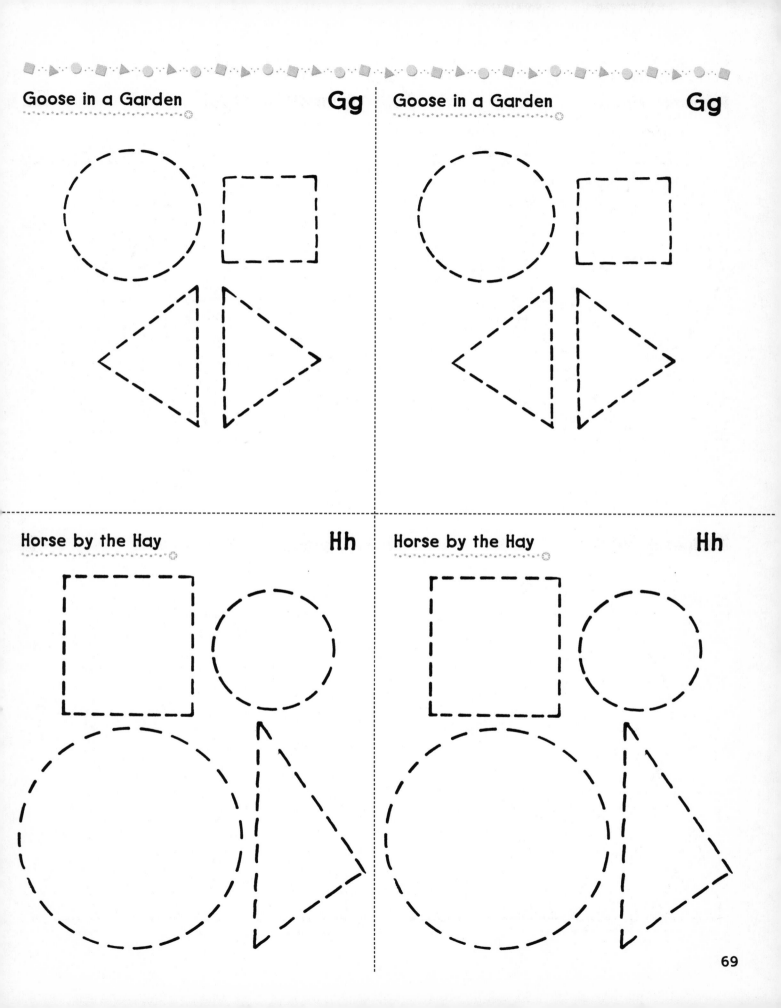

Goose in a Garden

Gg

Horse by the Hay

Hh

Horse by the Hay

Hh

Iguana in the Ivy

Ii

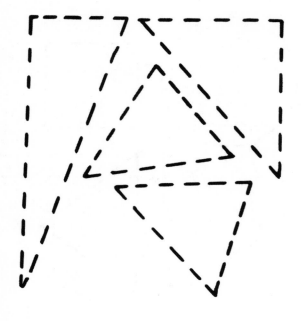

Iguana in the Ivy

Ii

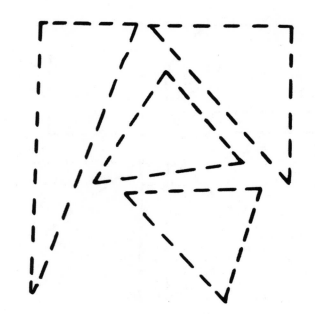

Jaguar in the Jungle

Jj

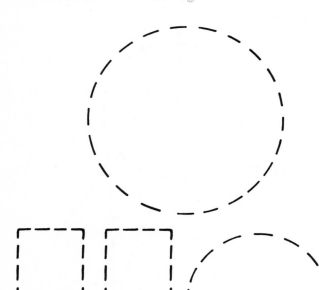

Jaguar in the Jungle

Jj

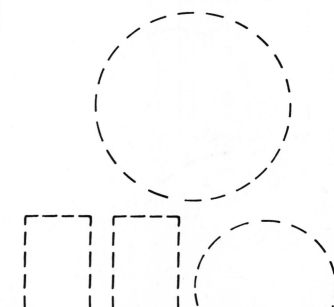

Kk

King with a Kite

Kk

Ladybug on a Leaf

Ll

Ladybug on a Leaf

Ll

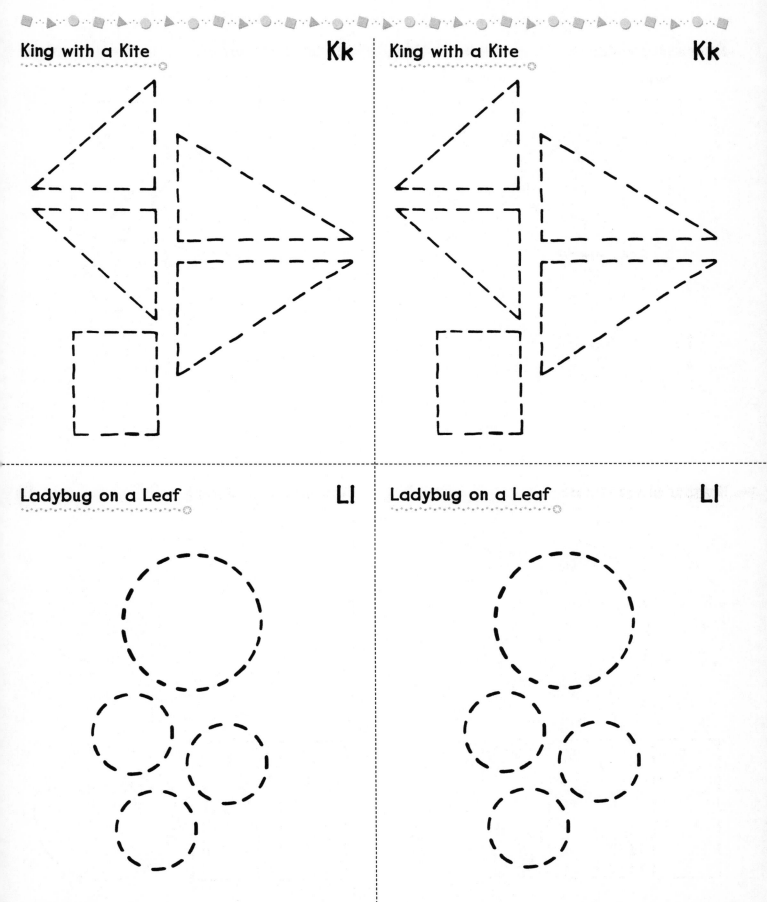

Mouse in a Meadow Mm

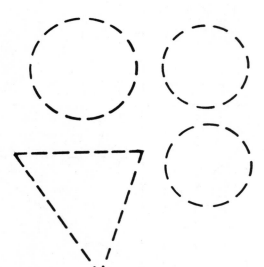

Mouse in a Meadow Mm

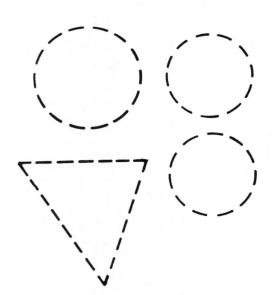

Nightingale in a Nest Nn

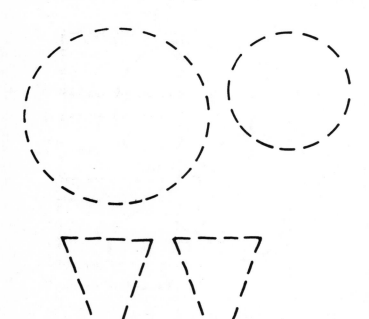

Nightingale in a Nest Nn

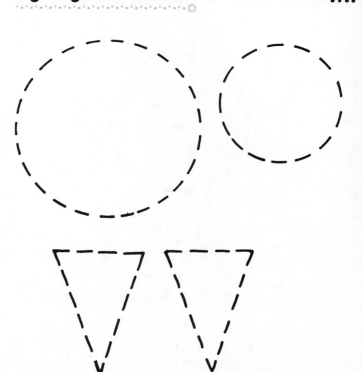

Pig in a Puddle **Pp**

Pig in a Puddle **Pp**

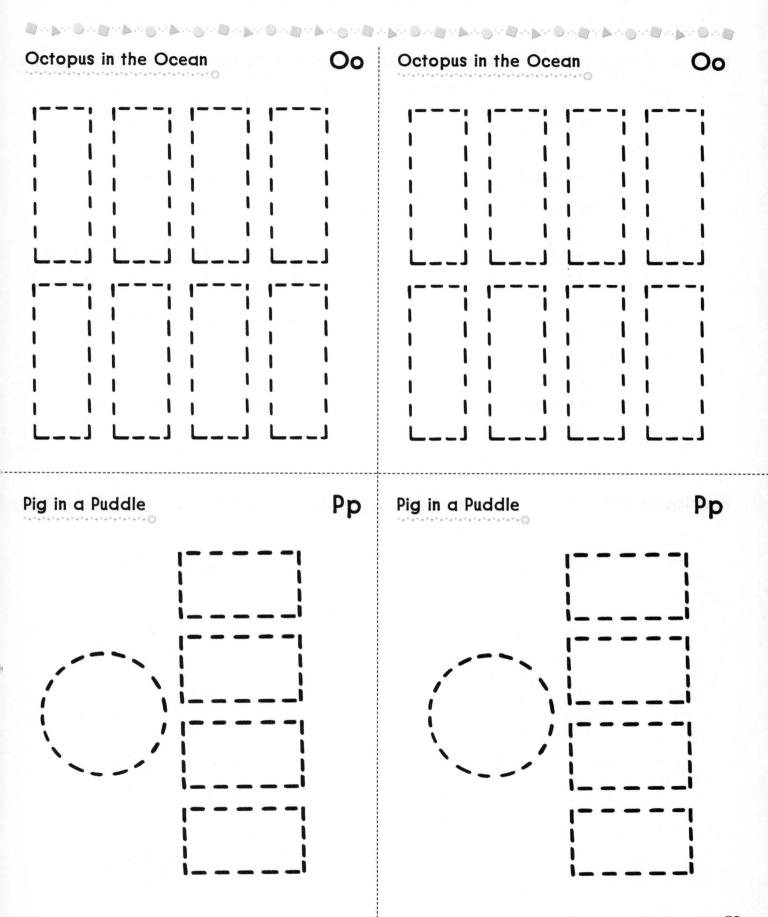

Quail on a Quilt   Qq

Quail on a Quilt   Qq

Rabbit by a River   Rr

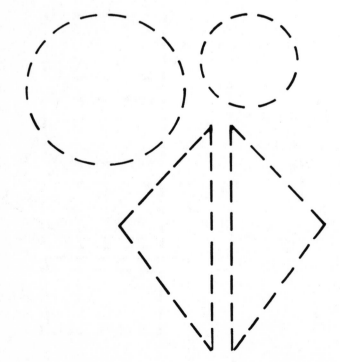

Rabbit by a River   Rr

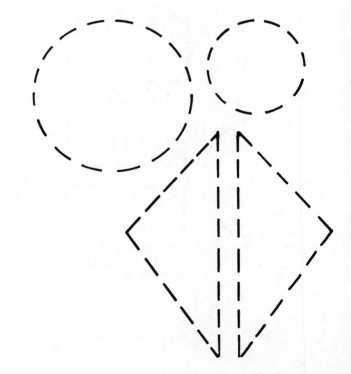

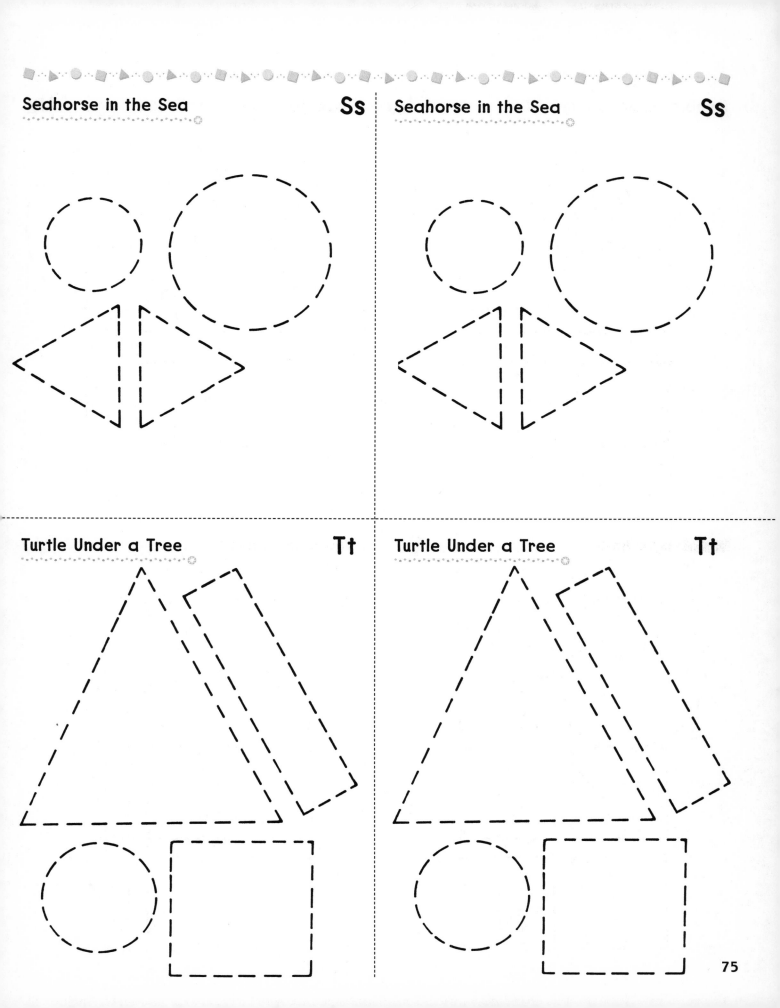

Seahorse in the Sea — Ss

Seahorse in the Sea — Ss

Turtle Under a Tree — Tt

Turtle Under a Tree — Tt

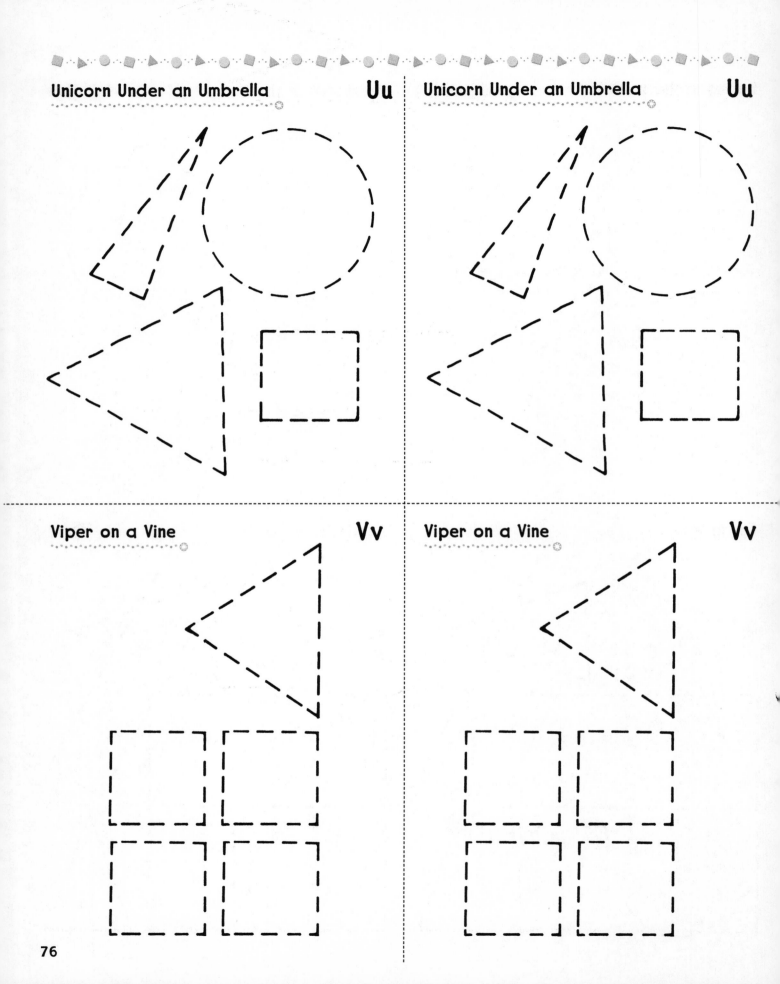

Unicorn Under an Umbrella

Uu

Unicorn Under an Umbrella

Uu

Viper on a Vine

Vv

Viper on a Vine

Vv

76

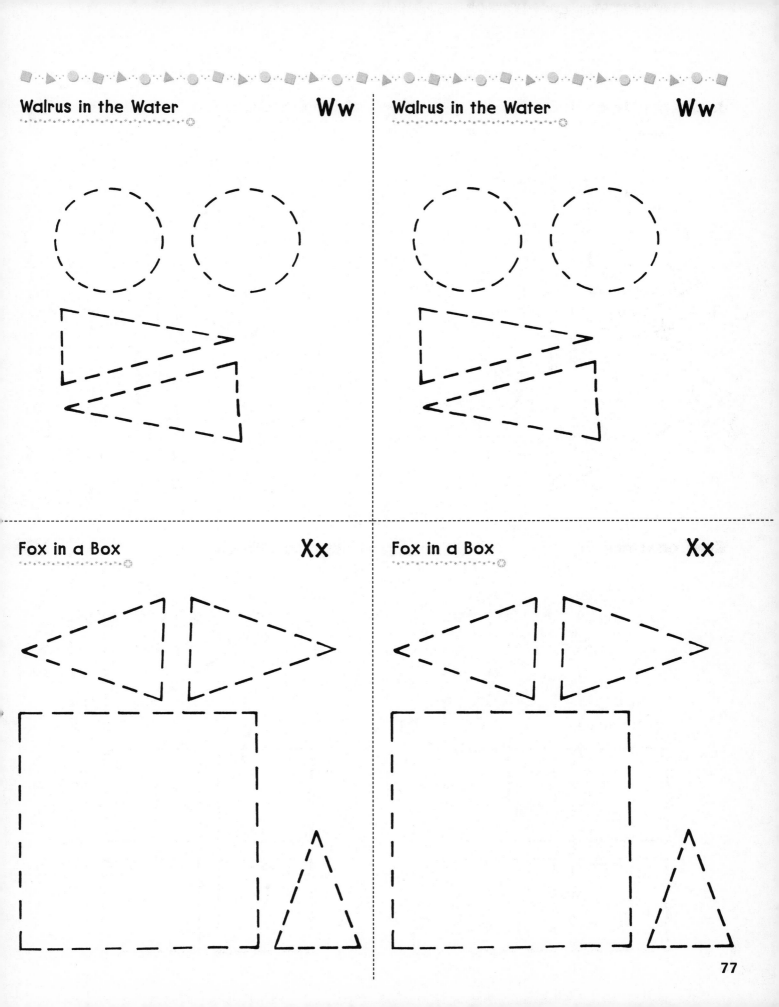

Walrus in the Water Ww

Walrus in the Water Ww

Fox in a Box Xx

Fox in a Box Xx

Yak in the Yard   **Yy**

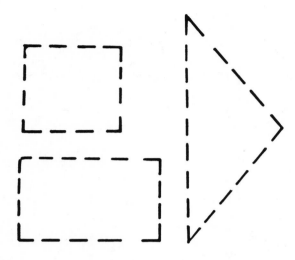

Yak in the Yard   **Yy**

Zebra at the Zoo   **Zz**

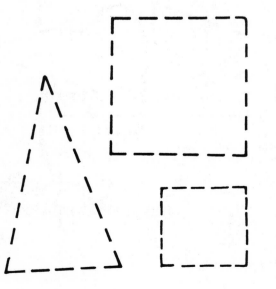

Zebra at the Zoo   **Zz**

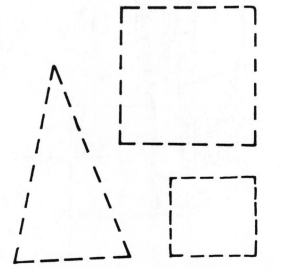

My Alphabet Shape Book

Name _____

Notes